FOR THE CARING PROFESSIONS

Other books in this series
by Sydney S. Chellen
AVAILABLE NOW FROM CASSELL

Information Technology for the Caring Professions: A User's Handbook
Word for Windows for the Caring Professions: A Beginner's Workbook

Watch for these forthcoming titles:
Minitab for the Caring Professions: A Beginner's Workbook
Word 6 for the Caring Professions: A Beginner's Workbook
Wordperfect for the Caring Professions: A Beginner's Workbook

FOR THE
CARING PROFESSIONS

A Beginner's Workbook

Sydney S. Chellen
M.Ed(Kent), BA(Ed), PGCE(FE), RNT, RCNT, RMN, RGN

with

Patricia D. Chellen
B.Ed (Hons), Dip. HE

CASSELL

Cassell   215 Park Avenue South
Wellington House   New York, NY 10003
125 Strand
London WC2R 0BB

First published 1996

British Library Cataloguing in Publication Data
A catalogue record of this book is available from the British Library.
ISBN: 0 304 33241 0

Disclaimer: Because the author has no control over the circumstances of use of this workbook, he cannot assume liability or responsibility for any consequential loss or damage, however caused, arising as a result of carrying out the exercises in the workbook. These materials are offered to the purchaser on the basis of this understanding.

All of the information in the workbook is believed to be correct at the time of printing. Whenever possible the author will try to assist with any queries.

Typeset using Word for Windows by: Sydney S.Chellen.
Printed and bound in Great Britain

Acknowledgements

A special thank you to reviewers from schools and colleges in the Kent area, and particularly to Marian Mifsud, and Patricia and Maurice Chellen, who gave generously of their time to test every step in this workbook before it went into print.

In most cases the left-hand pages are used to offer information and explanation which you should read **before** attempting any of the exercises.

All exercises can be found on the right-hand pages.

EXERCISE
Remember

On the far right of the EXERCISE page, you will find information that you should always keep in mind in order to make a particular feature work properly.

ATTENTION

This provides information and instructions that you must follow.

bold

Key terms and words you must type are written in **bold.**

italic

Some text are written in italic. They appear immediately after an instruction. They describe what is likely to happen after you have carried out the instruction. You should read the *italicized text* before carrying out the instruction.

This sign indicates that you should carry out the instructions listed, using the mouse EXCEPT where otherwise indicated.

HELP

Wherever you see this sign, you should find **additional assistance** to help you get out of difficult situations.

Warning

This is a **warning** sign to prevent possible loss of data or negative consequences.

*This workbook is dedicated
to my wife, Georgina, and my two brothers,
with deep affection*

---

*"Man is a tool using animal.
Without tools he is nothing.
With tools he is all."*
Thomas Carlyle

Table of Contents

Conventions   v

     ix

Assumptions

Excel for Windows   2

Using the mouse to issue commands   3

Short cuts in Excel   3

Using the keyboard to issue commands   4

Screen Pointer   5

Some keyboard buttons and their uses with Excel   6

LESSON 1	APPROXIMATELY 40-60 MINUTES	7-22
	Lesson objectives	7
Exercise 1	Loading Windows at the DOS C:\> prompt	9
Exercise 2	Starting the Windows tutorial	11
Exercise 3	Opening and closing Program Groups	13
Exercise 4	Starting an application eg, Write	13
Exercise 5	Making an application window occupy the full computer screen	15
Exercise 6	Reducing an open application into an icon	15
Exercise 7	Moving a window from one location to another	17
Exercise 8	Changing the width and height of a window (resizing)	17
Exercise 9	Revealing the contents of a menu	19
Exercise 10	Closing down applications	19
Exercise 11	Shutting down Windows	21
	ROUNDUP FOR LESSON 1	22

LESSON 2	APPROXIMATELY 50-60 MINUTES	23-40
	Lesson objectives	23
Exercise 1	Starting Excel for Windows 3.1	25
Exercise 2	Minimizing, Maximizing and Merging windows	27
Exercise 3	Switching ON/OFF the formatting, utility, drawing and chart tool bars	29
Exercise 4	Scrolling Up, Down, Right and Left	31
Exercise 5	Selecting cell or cells	33
Exercise 6	Entering data in the worksheet	35
Exercise 7	Inserting and deleting text or figures	37
Exercise 8	Saving an unnamed document to a floppy disk and hard disk	39
	ROUNDUP FOR LESSON 2	40

LESSON 3	APPROXIMATELY 50-60 MINUTES	41-58
	Lesson objectives	41
Exercise 1	Moving data to another cell and creating a series	43
Exercise 2	Removing unwanted data from cells	45
Exercise 3	Copying, cutting and pasting	47

Exercise	4	Retrieving and renaming a worksheet from a floppy disk	49
Exercise	5	Inserting and deleting rows in a worksheet	51
Exercise	6	Inserting and deleting columns in a worksheet	53
Exercise	7	Saving a named document	55
Exercise	8	Adjusting column widths	57
		ROUNDUP FOR LESSON 3	58

LESSON 4		**APPROXIMATELY 60-70 MINUTES**	**59-82**
		Lesson objectives	**59**
Exercise	1	Applying formulae to figures in a range of cells	61
Exercise	2	Testing the reliability of formulae	63
Exercise	3	Putting cell entries in bold and italics	65
Exercise	4	Increasing and decreasing font size	67
Exercise	5	Changing the font and point size	69
Exercise	6	Centring and aligning text	71
Exercise	7	Number and currency format	73
Exercise	8	Inserting borders and shades, and removing gridlines	75
Exercise	9	Spellchecking a worksheet	77
Exercise	10	Previewing a worksheet before printing	79
Exercise	11	Printing a worksheet	81
		ROUNDUP FOR LESSON 4	82

LESSON 5		**APPROXIMATELY 50-60 MINUTES**	**83-98**
		Lesson objectives	**83**
Exercise	1	Creating a new chart	85
Exercise	2	Updating, relocating and changing the embedded chart type	87
Exercise	3	Resizing and shifting between chart and worksheet	89
Exercise	4	Adding text to a chart	91
Exercise	5	Saving an embedded chart and closing down a file	93
Exercise	6	Creating a chart document	95
Exercise	7	Opening a chart document	97
		ROUNDUP FOR LESSON 5	98

LESSON 6		**APPROXIMATELY 40-50 MINUTES**	**100-109**
		Lesson objectives	**100**
Exercise	1	Creating and defining a database	101
Exercise	2	Maintaining a database (add, find, edit and delete records)	103
Exercise	3	Sorting the data in the database using 1st and 2nd keys	105
Exercise	4	Extracting records from the database	107
Exercise	5	Printing and Saving extracted records to disk	109

APPENDICES			**110-115**
	1	**Steps for formatting a disk using Windows Utility program**	110
	2	**Additional Toolbars for Excel version 5.0**	111
		Additional Toolbars for Excel version 4.0	112
		Description of the Tools on the Toolbars	113
	3	**Steps for creating a custom toolbar and adding icons to it.**	114
	4	**Troubleshooting**	115
	5	**Assignment: A sample Electronic Duty Sheet**	116
		Steps for creating the sample Electronic Duty Sheet	117

INDEX	**118**

Note to the reader

with spreadsheets. It introduces the user to
of a spreadsheet and some valuable techniques in creating and editing
worksheets.

Although Microsoft® EXCEL 4.0 & 5.0® in a Windows®environment is
being used here as the software on which you will learn to enter and
manipulate information in a spreadsheet, it is important to bear in mind
that there are several other equally good spreadsheet packages
available, such as Lotus 1,2,3® and QuattroPro®. However, the skills
acquired through using one spreadsheet package are invariably
transferrable to other packages.

The learning material in this workbook requires little or no assistance
from anyone else, and so it can be used as a self-instruction workbook.
However, once you have mastered the concepts contained in this
booklet, it is essential to start referring to the manual supplied with
Excel, and the on-screen tutorial which accompanies the program.

It goes without saying that, having worked your way through each
section, you will need to practise the skills that have been learnt by being
inventive and carrying out additional tasks. Only by so doing will the full
potential of this powerful and almost industry-standard spreadsheet be
realized.

How to use this workbook

This workbook is self-paced and provides an individualized, interactive learning package. The material is divided into six lessons. Each lesson is 40-70 minutes long and contains a series of exercises which are intended to be completed in one sitting. You should, therefore, ensure that you have the time needed prior to starting any of the lessons, particularly Lessons 2-6. Should it become necessary to stop a lesson prematurely, save the document if you can, **using your own filename**. This way you will be able to retrieve the file when you are ready to start the lesson again. Otherwise, exit the program without saving your work.

It is important that you follow the instructions and apply some common sense. For example, if you find that after having carried out an instruction you do not get the expected result, you should always try again as you may have accidentally done something wrong.

This workbook has been structured in such a way that each lesson builds on the previous ones.

- If you are a newcomer to Excel spreadsheet and you have not previously used a mouse under the Windows environment, you are strongly advised to start with Lesson 1 and work your way up from here. In order to ensure that you have fully developed the necessary skills needed to tackle ensuing exercises, you may need to repeat some of the exercises more than once before moving on.

- If you are familiar with Windows but new to Excel, you may like to start with Lesson 2, and then, work your way up slowly and methodically and do carry out all the exercises as suggested.

- If you are already familiar with Excel for Windows, but wish to practise certain aspects, you may like to go to selected pages and try out some of the exercises using your own document.

All exercises in this workbook appear on the right-hand page of a spread. These take you step-by-step through precise keystroke sequences to perform a series of tasks. Do resist the temptation of rushing to do the exercises before having first read the explanatory material on the INFO pages, which put these exercises in context. We have enjoyed putting the workbook together, and we hope you find it useful. We look forward to receiving your comments.

Sydney S. Chellen
Senior Lecturer Nursing Studies
Canterbury Christ Church College of
Higher Education
Canterbury, Kent.

Patricia D. Chellen
Teacher
Napier Primary School
Gillingham, Kent.

Introduction

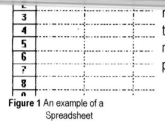

row intersect is a box usually referred to as cell. The cell is given two co-ordinates - the column letter followed by the row number. These cells may be filled with numbers (values), labels (text), and formulae (eg, the percentage).

Figure 1 An example of a
Spreadsheet

Uses for a spreadsheet in health care settings

There are many uses for Spreadsheets. The most obvious uses are for mathematical calculations and organization of figures such as planning and forecasting budgets. Like any business, Nursing and Nursing Education need to handle numerical data.

In health care, Spreadsheets can be used for
- budget control - financial forecast.
- stock control - ward stock of equipment, dressings, drugs, stationery etc.
- Scheduling of staff duties, holidays.

In Nursing Education too, Spreadsheets can be used for
- analysis of data - such as examination results, student intakes and wastage, or other research activities.
- scheduling of student placements or staff holidays
- budget control - eg, salaries, travel expenses.

Advantages of an Electronic Spreadsheet

For many years, Service and Education Managers have used large sheets of papers divided into columns and rows "spread out" on their desks to arrange information. Having spent hours writing various types of data in these columns and rows, Managers would then spend further time rearranging and analysing the data, and performing calculations, using formulae, adding text and drawing graphs. When the data changes, more time is spent making the necessary adjustments. Research has shown that 30 to 40 per cent of Nurses' and Nursing

Managers' time are spend on tedious paper work of this nature.

With the advent of computers, electronic Spreadsheet eliminates the need to use these large sheets of paper. It has ready-made columns and rows which can be easily and quickly adjusted to various lengths and widths (*see* Fig.1). The computer Spreadsheet also has an in-built facility to perform calculations.

The computer Spreadsheet is the perfect electronic tool or application program for handling some of the dreary tasks that take hours to do - ie, any information that can be represented as columns and rows. It is easier to use an electronic Spreadsheet than to perform calculations manually.

The advantages of Electronic Spreadsheets over manual ones can be summarized as follows:

- Speed calculations, hence quicker results.
- Minimize errors.
- Save time, hence user has more time to concentrate on other things.
- Increase output
- Reduce manpower cost

Assumptions

For the purposes of the lessons in this workbook, it is assumed that your PC has:

- a hard disk drive
- one floppy drive
- Windows 3.1 installed
- Excel 4.0, 4.0a or 5.0 installed
- multiple-button mouse - this will be held in your right hand and the LEFT button is configured as the primary button while the RIGHT button is set as the secondary button.

It is also assumed that when you switch on your computer, this sign: **C:\>** or **C:>** (known as the C prompt) will appear on your screen.

If, when you turn on your PC or the college computer you see something else, you should check with whoever set up the equipment for additional directions.

Excel for Windows

Excel for Windows is a powerful, flexible and easy to use spreadsheet package with excellent in-context help. This industry standard spreadsheet provides the caring professionals working in a variety of settings with the perfect automated business tool. Excel can be used to carry out a variety of tasks (*see page 1 - Uses of a spreadsheet in health care settings*).

buttons, the mouse's purpose is the same. It is there to move the **Screen pointer**, which is the arrow on the screen.

Screen pointer

Knowing how to use a mouse skilfully is very important because it will help you take full advantage of the applications running in Windows environments. For this reason, all the practise lessons in this workbook will, in most cases, concentrate on using the mouse, although it is quite possible but more cumbersome to perform most operations using the keyboard.

If you have never used a mouse before, you might have some difficulties initially, but with practice you are bound to improve your skills. The way to use the mouse is to hold it in your hand. Sliding the mouse on a flat surface in the desired direction and pressing the mouse button are the only two actions involved in the basic skills of **pointing, clicking** and **dragging.**

- When **pointing**, you should place the tip of the screen pointer over a specific item or area on the screen you want.
- A **click** is one quick press and release of the mouse button in a non-stop action <u>without</u> moving the mouse.
- When **double-clicking,** press and release the mouse button twice in rapid succession <u>without</u> moving the mouse.
- When **dragging,** press the mouse button and hold it down while moving the mouse; then release the button.

The program icons:

Excel 4.0

Microsoft
Excel 5.0

A Program Group icon:

Here are some examples:

1 To select a cell (eg, cell A1), you **point** to cell A1 and **click** the mouse button. (usually the LEFT mouse button).

2 To select an icon (which is a small picture representing a program or a program group), you **point** to that icon and **double-click** the mouse button.

3 To select a range of cells (eg, Cell A1 to B7), you **point** to cell A1, **click** the mouse button, then **drag** to cell B7.

Short cuts in Excel

Excel offers you several ways to carry out the same task, including short cuts. In this workbook we are going to take full advantage of these short cut facilities to speed learning.

When using a multiple-button mouse, all procedures in Excel can be carried out by just using the primary button (ie, the LEFT mouse button), as if it was a single-button mouse. However, some procedures can be carried out even faster by clicking the secondary button (ie, the RIGHT mouse button).

Most procedures in this workbook will require you to click the LEFT mouse button. When appropriate you will be asked to click the RIGHT button.

If you should inadvertently press the RIGHT mouse button instead of the LEFT, a list of commands will appear on the screen. To switch it off, you simply press ESCAPE key. You will find this key on the top-left hand corner of your keyboard.

Using the keyboard to issue commands

Commands can also be issued using keys on the keyboard, although in this workbook we are going to concentrate mostly on issuing commands using the mouse. Occasionally, I will be suggesting that you use certain keys on the keyboard if I think you might have difficulty issuing a particular command with the mouse. Some of the most vital keys on the keyboard are shown in Table 2 on page 6.

Screen Pointer

Arrow pointer leaning left	Sand-timer	Trans-parent cross	I-beam pointer		Double-headed arrows	Double-headed arrows with split bars	Double-headed arrows with horizontal and vertical bars	Plus-sign	Four-headed arrows	Magnify-ing glass

The **Pointer** is used to choose/select operations. Its shape changes as it moves over various areas of the screen. For example:

1 When on the menu bar, scroll bars, charts graphic objects, and when dragging cell contents between rows and columns on a worksheet, the Pointer changes to an **arrow leaning backwards** (ie, to the left).

2 When activating an application or carrying out an action, the Pointer takes the shape of a **Sand-timer**.

3 When the Pointer is resting on the working area of the spreadsheet, it takes the shape of **transparent-cross.**

4 When the Pointer is in the **Formula area** or text box it changes to an **I-beam** shape. The flashing cursor will appear where the I-beam cursor is, if you click the left mouse button indicating that typing can begin.

5 When the Pointer assumes the **double-headed horizontal arrow**, you can change the size of a window horizontally. When it changes to a **double-headed vertical arrow**, you can change the window size vertically.

6 When dividing a worksheet window into vertical or horizontal panes the Pointer changes to a **double-headed arrow with a vertical or horizontal split lines.**

7 When resizing the width of columns or height of rows, the Pointer changes to a **double-headed arrow with a solid vertical or horizontal line** respectively.

8 When filling a range of cells or creating a series on a worksheet, the Pointer changes to a thick **plus-sign.**

9 When you choose the split command from the document control menu, the Pointer changes to a **four-headed arrow with a window in the middle.**

10 When previewing pages before printing, the Pointer changes to a **magnifying glass**. When the Pointer assumes this shape you can click on the left mouse button to magnify the portion of the page for closer inspection.

Note: If the Pointer assumes a shape you don't want to use, or assumes an unexpected shape, press the ESC key on the keyboard, or move the Pointer to the middle of the worksheet and click the left mouse button. This should restore the Pointer to its usual shape.

Some keyboard buttons and their uses with Excel

Table 2

↑ ← ↓ →	**UP arrow** **LEFT arrow** **DOWN arrow** **RIGHT arrow**	These are the Screen pointer control keys. They can be used to move the Screen pointer or insertion point on the screen in the four directions indicated by the arrows.
←	**BACKSPACE**	This key is sometimes referred to as the DELETE key, because it allows you to move to the left on the screen, erasing characters as you go. This is an important key to use for making corrections.
↵	**ENTER**	This key is sometimes referred to as the RETURN key. In Excel it can be used to: • let the computer know that you want a particular instruction to be carried out instead of clicking the OK button. • transfer data from the Formula area to cells
TAB	**TAB**	This key is used to move the cursor from one column to another.
Ctrl	**Control**	This alters the meaning of some keys.
⇧	**SHIFT**	This key permits upper-case characters to be typed. It is also used to type the characters which rest above the numeric characters.
Alt	**ALTernate**	This is like the control key; it alters the meanings of some keys. You hold it down while simultaneously pressing other keys.
Esc	**ESCape**	This key can be used when you wish to stop using a procedure or get yourself out of trouble.
Num Lock	**Num Lock**	Before you can use the keypad (ie, the group of numeric keys to the right of the standard keyboard keys) the Num Lock light must be switched on. Use this toggle switch to turn the light ON and OFF.
Delete	**Delete**	Use this key to erase text lying to the right of the Cursor.

6

EXERCISE 1.1	1 recognize the DOS C:\> prompt; 2 load Windows at the DOS C:\ prompt;
EXERCISE 1.2	3 identify the Program Manager window and the <u>H</u>elp menu; 4 start the **<u>W</u>indows Tutorial**;
EXERCISE 1.3	5 identify **Program Group icons**; 6 open and close a Program Group;
EXERCISE 1.4	7 identify an **application program**; 8 start an application;
EXERCISE 1.5	9 state a possible danger of working with an application window that does not occupy the full screen; 10 make an application window occupy the full screen as required;
EXERCISE 1.6	11 differentiate between a program icon and a running application; 12 which has been iconized; 13 reduce an application which is being used into an icon;
EXERCISE 1.7	14 give a reason for wanting to move a window from one location to another; 15 move a window from one location to another;
EXERCISE 1.8	16 give a reason for wanting to change the size of a window; 17 resize a window as required;
EXERCISE 1.9	18 identify the **Menu bar** and **Menus** on any application; 19 expose the commands that are hidden behind a Menu on the Menu bar;
EXERCISE 1.10	20 identify the **control menu box**; 21 close down an application;
EXERCISE 1.11	22 close down Windows.

Using Microsoft® Windows

Excel is a Windows application. This means that before you can load Winword you must first load Microsoft Windows. **Windows** (written with an uppercase W) is the trademark of a product produced by an American company called Microsoft, whilst **windows** (written with a lowercase w) refers to frame areas of the computer screen. This section explains a few basic skills you need to know to work with the Windows environment.

☞ **GO TO page 23** - if you know Microsoft Windows and know how to load it.

📖 **DO READ ON** - if you are new to Microsoft Windows.

When you switch on a computer in which Windows has been installed, the setup on the machine you are using may be such that Windows is loaded automatically.

You will know that Windows has loaded if your screen resembles that of Fig.1.1

Figure 1.1 Program Manager window for Windows 3.1

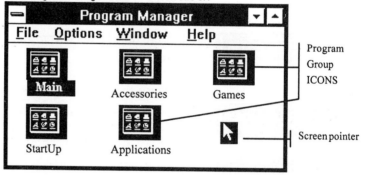

On the other hand, when you switch on your computer you may need to type the necessary command to load Windows. What command you type will depend on how the computer you are using has been set up. A college/institution network may have a menu system which comes on when the computer is first turned on. You may need to enter your password and username before you can use the system. There may also be menu options for starting Windows. You will need to check the local idiosyncrasy with regards to the loading procedure.

For the purposes of this lesson, I am assuming you have a hard disk and when you turn on your computer the **DOS C> prompt**, which looks like **C:\>** or **C:>**, appears.

🖥 **DO Exercise 1.1** - it will show you how to load Windows from the DOS prompt.

...in FRAME 1.1 if necessary. When you

DOS C:\>

❶ Switch on your **computer** and the **monitor**.
The computer will start a self-check procedure. Wait until this is completed before going to Step 2.

❷ Type your **username** and **password** as required, and press **any button** on the keyboard when/if instructed to do so. Otherwise, move to Step 3.
If you receive an error message, you may have entered the wrong password or username.

❸ At the **C** prompt type **WIN** then, press ENTER key(↵).
*After a few seconds Windows should load. If Windows is successfully loaded, you should be able to see the **Program Manager** window on your screen and it should more or less resemble that of Figure 1.1*

For computer and monitor switches look at the bottom right-hand or back of the base unit and monitor respectively.

 GO TO page 10 - if you can see the Program Manager.
■ **See HELP box** - if the Program Manager is not visible

HELP

- On some systems you may need to give extra information before you can start Windows. If you receive an error message when you do Step 3, then at the DOS prompt type **CD\WINDOWS** and press ENTER(↵), then type **WIN** and press ENTER(↵).
- Some systems, including college networks, may have a menu (ie, a list of options). In this case, follow the on-screen instructions.
- If you cannot get Windows started, please check the loading procedure with whoever set up your PC, or with the College Computer Manager/Information Technology Lecturer.

The Program Manager

Normally, when Windows is loaded, the Program Manager appears as an open window covering the whole screen. Occasionally, when Windows is loaded, all you can see on your screen is one tiny icon labelled Program Manager. In this case, you will need to open it into a window. This is done by steadying the **Screen pointer** on the Program Manager icon and double-clicking the left mouse button.

Figure 1.2 Showing an opened Program Manager window and an iconized Program Manager

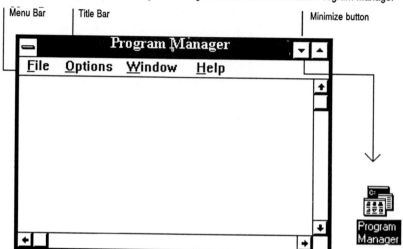

In order to use Windows and related applications effectively there are a few basic skills you need to develop. If the system you are using has Windows 3.1 installed, it may also contain a **Windows Tutorial** program hidden behind **Help**, which is located on the **Menu Bar** of the Program Manager window.

The tutorial has two useful lessons which you are strongly recommended to do:
*   Lesson 1 shows you how to use the mouse;
*   Lesson 2 shows you simple Windows features and helps you to develop a few basic but important skills.

☞ **GO TO page 12** - if this Windows Tutorial is not available to you then read on.
☞ **GO TO page 11** - and use the steps listed to activate the Windows Tutorial.

...4.2 below. If when you reach Step 2, you cannot

How to start the tutorial

❶ Steady the Screen pointer on **Help**, then click the left mouse button. *A pop-up menu containing a list of commands should appear.*

❷ Press **W** on the keyboard or steady the Screen pointer on the **Windows Tutorial** and click the left mouse button. *A welcome message should appear and the tutorial will start.*

❸ Press the letter **M** to start the mouse lesson. Follow on-screen instructions. When you have completed this lesson, then go on to Step 4.

❹ Steady the Screen pointer on the box next to **"Go on the Windows Basics"** and click on the left mouse button. *The Windows Basics lesson should start.*

❺ Now, follow on-screen instructions. When you have completed both lessons, steady the Screen pointer on the box next to the **"Exit the Tutorial"** and click the left mouse button. *A 'dialog' box should appear asking you to confirm your decision.*

❻ Press the letter **Y**. *The 'Program Manager' should now reappear.*

1. The tip of the **Screen pointer** must always be exactly on the item being selected.

2. A **click** means one quick press and release of the mouse button in a non-stop action without moving the mouse.

☞ **GO TO page 12** - if you want to refresh your memory on any aspects.

☞ **GO TO page 20** - if you want to proceed with something else.

 # Program Groups

Programs are organized into groups and superimposed on the Program Manager desktop window. Each group is represented by an icon called a **Program Group icon.** The Program Group icons are like folders and each group icon or folder contains several programs. When a group is opened, the programs it contains are displayed in a window. Figure 1.3 shows a Program Manager window with EIGHT Program Groups. SEVEN of them (namely: **StartUp, Main, Applications, Games, Microsoft Excel 4.0, Trio DataFax,** and **Aldus**) are closed, but the **Accessories** group is open. All the other Program Groups could be similarly opened. Thus, your screen might look somewhat different.

Notice that the **Accessories window** is also superimposed onto the **Program Manager window** and has its own **Title Bar, Minimize** and **Maximize buttons.**

You can open and close Program Groups as required. The procedure for doing this is simple.

Figure 1.3 Program Manager showing EIGHT Program Groups: SEVEN closed, ONE open.

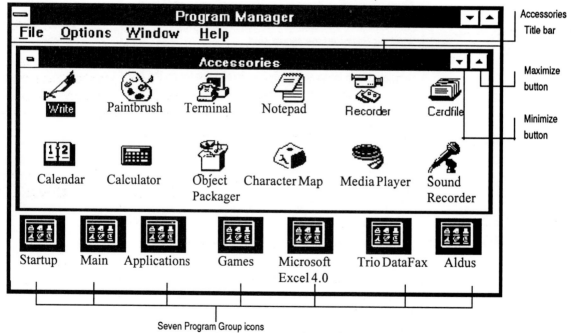

DO Exercises

1.3 and 1.4 - they offer practice in handling Program Groups and application.

...ing in opening and closing a Program Group.

Program Groups

❶Look at the **Program Manager** on your screen. If the **Accessories Program Group** is open, please skip Step 2.

❷ Steady the Screen pointer on the **Accessories Program Group icon**, and **double-click** the left mouse button. *This should open the Accessories Program Group, displaying what it contains.*

❸ Steady the Screen pointer on the **Minimize** button of the **Accessories group window** and click the left mouse button. *This should reduce the Accessories Program Group back to an icon.*

Always click the button of the appropriate window.

 **EXERCISE 1.4**

Write is a simple word processing program. It is one of several application programs likely to have been installed in the computer you are using. The procedure for starting an application program under Windows environment is quite simple and common to all. This exercise is designed to show you how to start the application Write. Please follow the steps listed in FRAME 1.4. Once Write is on your screen, **do not** be tempted to do anything else. Turn to the next page and start reading the information given there.

FRAME 1.4

| | **How to start an application eg, Write** | |

❶Look at the **Program Manager** on your screen. If the **Accessories Program Group** is open, please skip Step 2.

❷ Steady the Screen pointer on the **Accessories Program Group icon**, and **double-click** the left mouse button. *This should open the Accessories Program Group, displaying what it contains.*

❸ Steady the Screen pointer on the **Write** icon and **double-click** the left mouse button. *This should start Write and it should be ready for use in its own window.*

Remember

The Write program icon looks like this:

Write

 # Working with an application

When working with any application, it is prudent to make the application program window you are using occupy the full computer screen. This helps to prevent unforced errors. If an application is not occupying the full screen, this can be rectified by maximizing the window for that application. Maximizing a window enlarges it to cover the full computer screen.

Windows allows you to work with several applications at the same time. While working with one application you can temporarily reduce the other open applications to an **icon.** This helps free space on the screen without the need to close the application down. When a running application window has been reduced to an icon, it appears at the bottom of the screen.

Figure 1.4 Location of the Minimize and Maximize buttons on the Write application program

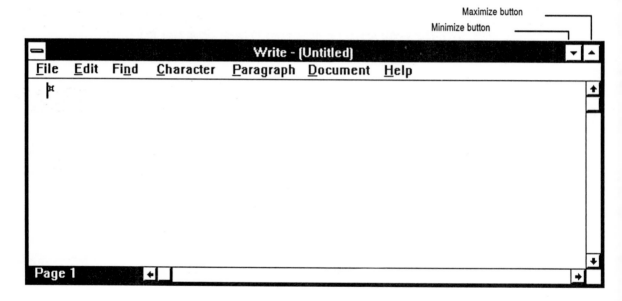

Any application that runs under a Windows environment can be **Maximized** and **Minimized** as required. However, inadvertent use of these buttons (Fig.1.4), particularly the minimize button, can be annoying, as you might see your work suddenly disappear without realizing what you have done. However, it is easy to recall, by **double-clicking** in the icon so that you reopen the application program window.

DO Exercises

1.5 and 1.6 - to experience what the Maximize and Minimize buttons do.

...ctice using the **Maximize** button. Try

❶ Ensure the **Write** program is open.

❷ Look at your monitor and see if the **Write** program is occupying the full computer screen. If it is, skip Step 3 and go to Exercise 1.6.

❸ Steady the Screen pointer on the **Maximize** button of the **Write** window, then click the left mouse button. *The Write program enlarges to occupy the full screen.*

already occupying the full screen, clicking the maximize button will have no effect.

 EXERCISE 1.6 Clicking on the **Minimize** button of any application window reduces it to an icon. This exercise offers you practice in using this button. Follow the steps in FRAME 1.6, then move on.

FRAME 1.6

	How to reduce an open application to an icon	

❶ Ensure the **Write** program is fully open.

❷ Steady the Screen pointer on the **Minimize** button (see Fig. 1.4), then click the left mouse button.
*The Write window reduces to an icon. You should be able to see two **Write** icons. One in the Accessories window and the other (ie, the one you minimized) at the bottom of the screen. **Notice** the one you minimized is labelled slightly differently from the other. If you have difficulty finding the second Write icon, then please read the help box below*

Remember

The procedure being used with **Write** is the same for any other application.

 HELP

- Sometimes, especially when other windows are occupying the entire screen, an application icon may be wholly or partially hidden under the other open windows. In such a situation, to get at the icon you are searching for, try closing or minimizing the possible offending window(s) or the Program Manager window itself.

- Do not be frightened to experiment with opening or closing windows. Rest assured that you are not likely to damage the computer system. The worst thing that could happen is that you lose your data. Losing data is part of the learning process, although you should try not to make a habit of it.

Relocating a window

Any window (which is not fully maximized) can be moved to another part of the screen. This is very useful, especially when trying to find a hidden icon, or when arranging icons or windows on the **Program Manager desktop.**

The width and height of a window can also be changed.

Figure 1.5

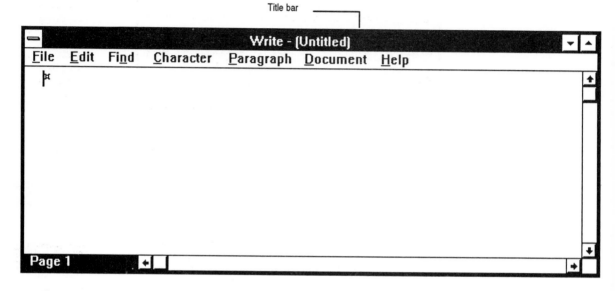

☐ **DO Exercises**
   1.7 and 1.8 - to practise moving windows and changing their size.

the flexibility of windows and give you

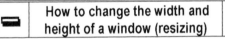 How to move a window from one location to another		

❶ Ensure the **Write** program is open.

❷ Steady the Screen pointer on the **Title bar** of **Write's** window, then **drag** ie, press and hold down the left mouse button and move the title to your chosen new location, then let go of the mouse button. (*Read* **HELP** *below*)

❸ Repeat Step 2 until you have the hang of it, then move on to the next exercise.

You minimized a **Write** icon in Exercise 1.6 which should be at the bottom of your screen. To reopen it just **double-click** that icon.

 EXERCISE 1.8 As already pointed out, being able to resize a window is an important skill. Carry out the steps in FRAME 1.8.

FRAME 1.8

How to change the width and height of a window (resizing)	▼	▲

❶ Ensure the **Write** program is open.

❷ Move the Screen pointer slowly over the **border**. When the pointer changes to a **double-headed** arrow, **drag** the border inwards or outwards until the window is the size you want. (*Read* **HELP** *below*).

❸ Repeat Step 2 until you have the hang of it, then move on to the next exercise.

Remember

The **double-headed** arrow looks like this :

HELP	• If the window of the **Write** program is occupying the full screen, then it is not possible to move it about, or to resize it.
	• In this situation try locating the restore button ⬍ . You should find it at the top-right corner of the screen, and click on it.

Menus

Almost all windows have a **Menu bar.** The Menu bar shows names of menus. Behind each menu there are several commands pertaining to the particular application in use. When a particular menu is opened, an extended list of commands is displayed as shown in Figure 1.6.

Figure 1.6 An extended list of commands from **File** menu

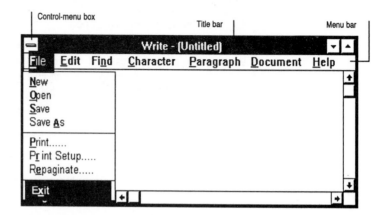

Figure 1.7 The Dialog box for Print command

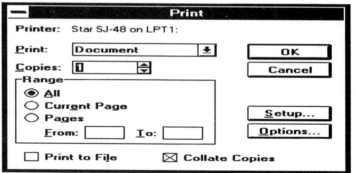

When commands are chosen, a **Dialog box** appears because more information is required. The Dialog box in Fig. 1.7 appears whenever you want to print your document onto paper. After supplying the information you simply click the **OK** button and the computer will carry out your instructions. Notice the **Cancel** button. If you've pressed the wrong button by mistake and a Dialog box appears, simply click on the cancel button once and you will be taken a step back.

DO Exercises
1.9 and 1.10 - to practise opening menus and closing down applications.

...practice in opening menus. If you are new

FRAME 1.9

| | How to reveal the contents of a menu | |

❶ Ensure that the **Write** program is open.

❷ Steady the tip of the Screen pointer on the command **File,** then click the left mouse button once. *An extended list of commands should appear.*

❸ Steady the Screen pointer anywhere on the **Title bar,** then click the left mouse button once again. *The extended list of commands should **vanish.**.*

Remember

Write is a word processor, though not as sophisticated as Word for Windows.

There are several ways of closing down an application. This exercise offers you one of the ways. Carry out the steps in FRAME 1.10.

FRAME 1.10

| | How to close down an application | |

❶ Identify the **Control Menu box** (see Fig. 1.6) of the application you want to close down. (**Do not** close the Program Manager window yet).

❷ Steady the Screen pointer on that box, then **double-click** the left mouse button. *That particular application should now close down. If a dialog box appears see* **HELP** *box below*

❸ Repeat Steps 1 and 2 with other applications you may have on your screen, except for the Program Manager.

Remember

If a **Save** dialog box should appear, click on the **YES** button to save your work.

HELP

• Whenever you are closing down an application, Windows makes a point of reminding you to save your work. If you do not want to save anything, then click on the **NO** button, otherwise click on the **YES** button.

 **INFO**

Shutting down Windows

Before turning off your computer, you should always quit Windows. The procedure for doing this is very simple as you shall see when you do Exercise 1.11. Here are two good reasons why you should always close Windows before switching off your computer:

1   As you become skilful in using Windows you will most certainly be using more than one application at a time. In such a situation you can easily forget to save all your work. By getting into the good habit of closing Windows down before switching off your computer, Windows will remind you of any works you have not saved.

2   Each time you use an application under Windows, it creates and saves on your hard disk temporary files for its own use. Windows will automatically delete these files from the hard disk when you shut it down. If you turn off your computer without first closing down Windows, these temporary files will remain on your hard disk occupying valuable space unnecessarily.

Figure 1.8 The Program Manager window

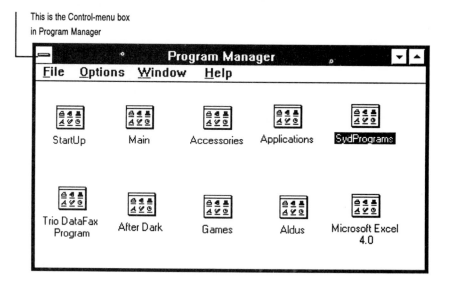

Take a look at Figure 1.8 and identify the Control-Menu box, before starting the exercise.

💻 **DO Exercise 1.11**   - it will show you the steps for shutting down Windows.

Follow the steps listed in FRAME 1.11 and

Windows

❶ Identify the **Control-menu** box for the Program Manager.

❷ Steady the Screen pointer on that box, then **double-click** the left mouse button. *A message should appear in a Dialog box reminding you that you are exiting Windows.*

❸ Steady the Screen pointer on the command **OK** and click the left mouse button.

Windows should now shut down, unless you have forgotten to save your work, in which case another Dialog box will appear asking what you want to do. (see **HELP box** *below)· .*

❹ When the **DOS** prompt appears remove any floppy disk you may have in the disk drive and switch off the computer and monitor.

Some people and organizations keep their computer on all the time. Do familiarise yourself with local rules when you are not using your own machine.

HELP

- Windows always keeps a watchful eye on all the programs you are using and it assumes you want to save all your work to disk. For any work that has not been saved, you will be asked if you want to save it. If you do, click on **YES**, otherwise click on **NO**.
- If you have, say, six applications running, Windows will ask the same question six times, one for each application.

1 Whenever Windows is loaded, the Program Manager appears either as an open window occupying the whole screen or as an icon.

2 The Program Manager is used to organize programs into groups. Each group is represented by a Program Group icon, which acts like a folder.

3 A Program or Program Group icon is selected on the screen by pointing the tip of the Screen pointer to it and then clicking the mouse button (usually the LEFT button).

4 When a Program Group is open the programs it contains are displayed in their own window which is superimposed onto the Program Manager window.

5 Basic mouse and Windows techniques can be learnt by using the on-line Windows Tutorial. This program can be started by choosing Windows Tutorial from the Program Manager's Help menu. However, the exercises in this section cover most of the necessary principles to work with Windows for those who do not have or do not wish to use the on-line Windows Tutorial.

6 Windows allows several applications/programs to be run at the same time. A running program can be iconized to free space on the Program Manager desktop, thus eliminating the need to close that application altogether.

7 Almost all windows have a **Menu bar.** The Menu bar shows names of menus. Behind each menu there are several commands pertaining to the particular application in use.

8 The arrangement of a program window on the screen, such as its size and location, can be altered as required by using the drag technique.

Before we close down this lesson remember two more points.

- When using Microsoft Windows and any application running under Windows, each open window is like a sheet of paper. Just as several sheets of paper can be layered one on top of the other or placed next to each other, several windows can be open at the same time, each one superimposed on the other or arranged next to one another.

Warning

- Each time Windows is used, several temporary files are created and written to the hard disk, thus occupying vital space. Windows will automatically get rid of those unwanted files, provided you exit Windows before switching off the computer. If you are not sure how to close down Windows, please follow the steps in Exercise 1.11

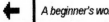 At the end of this lesson you should be able to: ▼ ▲	
EXERCISE 2.1	1 list ten facilities that Excel offers; 2 start Excel for Windows;
EXERCISE 2.2	3 identify the following: **Minimize, Maximize and Restore buttons**; 4 minimize, maximize and merge the worksheet with the Excel window;
EXERCISE 2.3	5 identify the following: **Title bar, Menu bar, Standard Toolbar, Formula bar and column headings**; 6 switch ON and Off the **Formatting, Utility, Drawing** and **Chart** Tool bars;
EXERCISE 2.4	7 identify the following: the **working area,** the **Scroll bars**; 8 scroll up, down, left and right;
EXERCISE 2.5	9 identify the following: a **cell**; 10 select a cell or a range of cells;
EXERCISE 2.6	11 identify the **Formula area**; 12 enter data in a worksheet; 13 correct noticeable typing mistakes immediately, using the BACKSPACE key on the keyboard;
EXERCISE 2.7	14 differentiate between an **Insertion point** and a **Screen pointer**; 15 insert and delete data in a worksheet;
EXERCISE 2.8	16 state the minimum number of characters acceptable for a filename; 17 name a new document; 18 save a new document to a floppy or hard disk.

[1] *Formatting:* A disk must be formatted before you can use it to save your work. If you do not know how to format a disk, then please refer to appendix 1.

INFO

Excel for Windows

For your information, here is a list of the facilities you can expect to find in Excel for Windows.

- **Autofill.** Excel has the ability to continue any series of numbers, dates, or month names you have started. Series are quickly created by dragging the Fill-handle (ie, the small solid square situated in the lower-right corner of the thick rectangular border which surrounds a selected cell), through a selection of cells.

- **Zooming views.** With the Zoom In and Zoom Out tools you can view your worksheets at different levels of magnification. The Zoom In tool allows you to focus more closely on a specific area of your worksheet while the Zoom Out tool enables you to view a larger area of the worksheet.

- **Moving and copying data with the mouse.** Contents of cells can be easily moved or copied to another location, by simply dragging the thick border surrounding cells that have been selected. This is a very useful facility. It helps to speed up data entries and corrections.

- **Spellcheck.** Text in your worksheets, macro sheets and charts can be quickly checked for spelling errors. New words can also be added to the spellchecking 'dictionary'.

- **Centring Text over Columns.** Using the alignment command on the Format menu, text over a selection of columns can be quickly centred.

- **Vertical Text in Cells.** Using the alignment command on the Format menu you can control the vertical or horizontal appearance of text in cells.

- **Analysis ToolPak Functions and Procedures.** Using the 'Analysis ToolPak' you can apply statistical analyses to many types of data.

- **ChartWizard.** With the 'ChartWizard' tool you can choose your chart type and format, and you can change the way data is plotted. Also, you can easily add a legend and title.

- **Crosstab ReportWizard.** Information in the fields of a database can be quickly compared and summarized by using the crosstab tables. The Crosstab ReportWizard prompts you with a series of choices, which require you to specify which data you want to include in the table and how you want various sets of data compared with each other.

- **Import and Export facilities.** Charts or graphs created using Excel can be easily imported into a document being created by Word.

Excel is easy to use, it has excellent in-context help and has a nice look and feel to it. To learn how to switch on Excel please do Exercise 2.1

When using a network, Excel takes longer to load. Once the Sand-timer

 EXERCISE 2.1 Load Excel. Follow the steps listed in FRAME 2.1 if necessary. When you have done so, move to the next page.

FRAME 2.1

How to load Excel from the Program Manager

❶ Load Windows. (For help, please refer to FRAME 2.1, p9).

❷ Identify the **Excel program** icon (see picture on the right. Notice that the icon for Version 4.0 is slightly different to that of version 5.0). *To find it, you may need to* **double-click** *on one of the following* **Program Group** *icons:* *Microsoft Excel 4.0 (or 5.0),* *Accessories,* *Applications,* *or other program group icons.*

❸ Steady the pointer on the **Excel program** icon and **double-click** the left mouse button.

The Screen pointer should change to a Sand-timer (⧖) and after a few seconds, Excel should load displaying a blank worksheet (see Figures 2.1 and 2.2, p26).

N.B. *If you are using* **Microsoft Office**, *then you should look at the top-right hand corner of your screen. You may find something like this:*

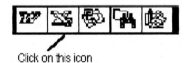

Click on this icon

Remember

1. The **Excel program** icon for version 5.0 looks like this:

Microsoft Excel 5.0

2. The **Excel program** icon for version 4.0 looks like this:

Microsoft Excel

3. The Excel **program-group** icon on version 4.0 looks like this:

Microsoft Excel 4.0

The Excel worksheet

NOTE
For Excel version
4.0 the smaller
window is called
Sheet1
instead of
Book1.

As Excel is started, a new empty spreadsheet (worksheet) is automatically opened for data to be entered. The Excel 5.0 spreadsheet may start off with two windows - one superimposed on the other - as in Fig. 2.1. Notice that the larger window shown here with the grey title bar is called the 'Microsoft Excel' window and the smaller window with the black title bar is the 'Book1' window. Both windows may be already merged together with only one title bar as in Fig. 2.2.

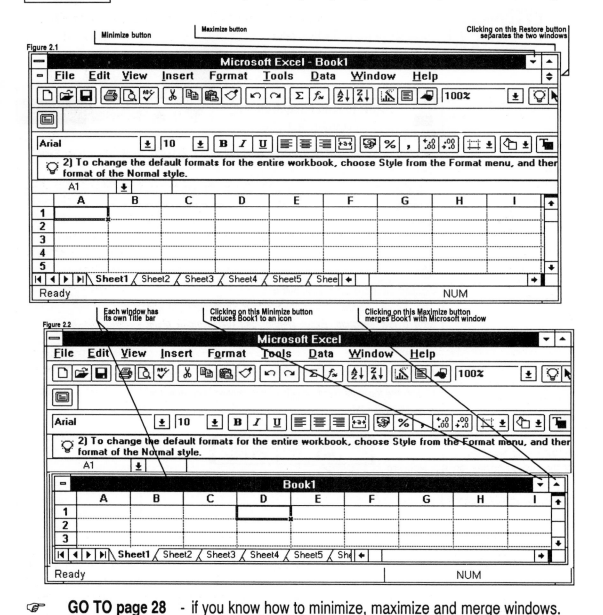

☞ **GO TO page 28** - if you know how to minimize, maximize and merge windows.
🖥 **DO Exercise 2.2** - and practise minimizing, maximizing and merging windows.

Remember

[b] Before moving on, please ensure that your work sheet looks like Fig. 2.1. (You may need to click the **Maximize** button on the '**Microsoft Excel**' window to make it occupy the entire screen).

FRAME 2.1

| How to reduce, open Microsoft Excel window | |

❶To reduce the '**Microsoft Excel-Book1**' or '**Microsoft Excel-Sheet1**' window to an icon
Steady the Screen pointer on the **Minimize** button (see Fig. 2.1) and click the left mouse button. *The Excel window should reduce to an icon.*
NOTE: *You should now be able to see two Excel program icons. One called 'Microsoft Excel' and the other 'Microsfot Excel-Book1' or 'Microsoft Excel-Sheet1', which is the one you minimized and it should be at the bottom of the screen towards the left corner (read HELP below).*

❷To open the '**Microsoft Excel-Book1**' or '**Microsoft Excel-Sheet1**' icon into a window
Steady the Screen pointer on the '**Microsoft Excel**' icon you minimized and **double-click** the left mouse button (or click the left mouse button, then press ENTER). *The Microsoft Excel - Book1 or Sheet1 window should open.*

❸To separate the '**Book1**' or '**Sheet1**' from the '**Microsoft Excel**' window
Steady the Screen pointer on the **Restore** button (see Fig. 2.2) and click the left mouse button. *The Book1 or Sheet1 window should separate from the Microsoft Excel window.*

FRAME 2.2

| How to reduce, open and merge Book1/Sheet1 window | |

❶To reduce the '**Book1/Sheet1**' window into an icon
Steady the Screen pointer on the **Minimize** button of the **Sheet1** window (see Fig. 2.2) and click the left mouse button. *Book1/Sheet1 only should reduce to an icon.*

❷To open '**Book1/Sheet1**'icon into a window
Steady the Screen pointer on the '**Book1/Sheet1**' icon, and **double-click** the left mouse button (or click the left mouse button, then press ENTER). *The Book1/Sheet1 window should open.*

❸To merge '**Book1/Sheet1**' window with the '**Microsoft Excel window.**'
Steady the Screen pointer on the **Maximize** button of the '**Book1/Sheet1**' window (see Fig. 2.2) and click the left mouse button. *Book1/Sheet1 window and the Microsoft Excel window should merge into one (Fig.2.1).*

HELP

If you cannot see the '**Microsoft Excel-Book1**' icon (or '**Microsoft Excel-Sheet1**', if you are using Excel version 4.0) at the bottom of your screen (near the left hand corner), it may be partially hidden under other opened windows. Try minimizing the Program Manager window and then check. You may need to close all offending windows to find your icon. Be careful and vigilant.

The Excel worksheet (contd)

As Excel is loaded, the first thing you should notice is that the worksheet looks like a window with similar features to other windows. You should be able to see at least two familiar features:

- The **Title bar** which displays the Control-menu box, title, and the Maximize and Minimize buttons.
- The **Menu bar** displaying several menus and Restore buttons.

Take a look at the Figure 2.3 below. They are some of the features that you will normally encounter on the horizontal bars at the top of the worksheet when Excel is loaded. (The wording on the Title and Menu bars, and the icons available on the Standard Toolbar for Excel version 4.0 are slightly different).

Figure 2.3 Horizontal bars on top of the Excel worksheet for Versions 4.0 and 5.0

① **The Title bar**
It displays the title of the worksheet

Maximize button

Control-menu box

Microsoft Excel

Minimize button

② **The Menu bar**
It shows a list of menu options. Hidden behind each option is a list of commands.

Restore button

Version 4.0

Restore button

| **File** | **Edit** | **Formula** | **Format** | **Data** | **Options** | **Macro** | **Window** | **Help** |

Version 5.0

Restore button

| **File** | **Edit** | **View** | **Insert** | **Format** | **Tools** | **Data** | **Window** | **Help** |

Restore button

③ **The Standard Toolbar**
It offers a shortcut to carrying out some of the commonest tasks.

Version 4.0

| Normal |

Version 5.0

100%

④ **Formula bar**
What you type will initially appear in the formula bar.

Version 4.0

A1

Reference Area

Formula Area

Version 5.0

A1

There are other tool bars that are not normally displayed when Excel is loaded but can be activated by clicking the <u>right</u> mouse button. You will be introduced to four of them namely: Formatting, Utility, Drawing and Chart. No drawings are shown here (*see* Appendix 2.)

☞ **GO TO page 30** — if you know how to switch ON and OFF additional Tool bars.

💻 **DO Exercise 2.3** — and practise switching ON and OFF additional Tool bars.

...some of them may be switched ON when you

 EXERCISE 2.3

FRAME 2.0 gives you toolbars on and off.

[a] Look at your screen. You should, at least, see the **Standard Toolbar**. If this is **not** the case, do the following:

For Excel version 4.0 click on these commands:
Options, Toolbars, Standard, Show

For Excel version 5.0 click on these commands:
View, Toolbars, Standard, OK

[b] Using the steps in FRAME 2.3 below, practise switching the Formatting, Utility, Drawing and Chart toolbars ON and OFF.

[c] Ensure all **Toolbars** (except for the Standard Tool bar), are switched OFF, before moving on.

1. Whenever a command on an extended-menu list is active it will show a √ before it.

2. Always use the LEFT mouse button unless you are instructed otherwise.

FRAME 2.3

How to display or hide the:			
Formatting toolbar	**Utility toolbar**	**Drawing toolbar**	**Chart toolbar**
❶ Steady the Screen pointer anywhere on the **Standard Toolbar** and click the **RIGHT** mouse button. *A list of commands should appear.*	❶ Steady the Screen pointer anywhere on the **Standard Toolbar** and click the **RIGHT** mouse button. *A list of commands should appear.*	❶ Steady the Screen pointer anywhere on the **Standard Toolbar** and click the **RIGHT** mouse button. *A list of commands should appear.*	❶ Steady the Screen pointer anywhere on the **Standard Toolbar** and click the **RIGHT** mouse button. *A list of commands should appear.*
❷ Steady the Screen pointer on the command **Formatting** and click the left mouse button.	❷ Steady the Screen pointer on the command **Utility** and click the left mouse button.	❷ Steady the Screen pointer on the command **Draw** and click the left mouse button.	❷ Steady the Screen pointer on the command **Chart** and click the left mouse button.
• *If the **Formatting** Tool bar was not visible it should pop up.* • *If the **Formatting** Toolbar was visible it should have disappeared.*	• *If the **Utility** Tool bar was not visible it should pop up.* • *If the **Utility** Tool bar was visible it should have disappeared.*	• *If the **Drawing** Tool bar was not visible it should pop up.* • *If the **Drawing** Tool bar was visible it should have disappeared.*	• *If the **Chart** Toolbar was not visible it should pop up.* • *If the **Chart** Tool bar was visible it should have disappeared.*
❸ Repeat Steps 1 and 2 to **reverse** the process.	❸ Repeat Steps 1 and 2 to **reverse** the process.	❸ Repeat Steps 1 and 2 to **reverse** the process.	❸ Repeat Steps 1 and 2 to **reverse** the process.

Each Excel worksheet is a rectangular grid. The intersection of each column and row is called a cell, in which data is stored. Each cell is referred to, by a letter and a number (as in a street map). As Figure 2.4 shows, each column of the worksheet has a letter and each row has a number. Thus the first column is labelled A, the second column is labelled B and so on. While the first row is labelled 1, the second row is labelled 2 and so on. Therefore:

- cell A1 is the first column of the first row
- cell A2 is the first column of the second row and so on.
- cell B1 is the second column of the first row
- cell B2 is the second column of the second row and so on.

Since the Excel worksheet has a total of 255 columns across, and 16,384 rows down (255 x 16,384 = 4,177,920 cells in total), the computer screen is not big enough to show all the rows and columns. At best you are likely to see 20 rows and 9 columns in one screen or window. A full sheet of data will spread over several of these windows. Hence the term Spreadsheet.

To move around various parts of the worksheet and view hidden rows or columns, you will need to roll the worksheet up or down, left or right. There are several ways of rolling the worksheet in various directions.

Figure 2.4 - Excel Worksheet for version 5.0

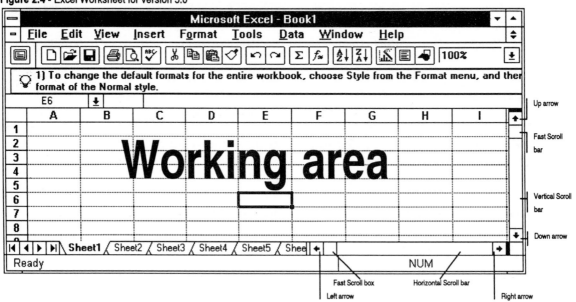

💻 **DO Exercise 2.4** - if you want to practise scrollling a worksheet.

...in FRAME 2.4, practise scrolling your worksheet UP

2   Hold down CTRL key and...
   Up,

3   Press the following keys: **TAB, TAB, TAB, ↓ , ← , ← , ← ,Page Up**.

FRAME 2.4

How to scroll a worksheet UP or DOWN   ▼ ▲

❶ Steady the tip of the Screen pointer on the **DOWN ↓** arrow button (of the **Vertical scroll bar**, Fig.2.4) then click the left mouse button **once**. *The worksheet scrolls up revealing one more row.*

❷ Click the **DOWN ↓** arrow again. *The worksheet moves up one more row.*

❸ Keep the Screen pointer on the **DOWN ↓** arrow and **hold down** the left button of the mouse. *You should see the worksheet scrolling continuously upwards revealing more rows.*

❹ Steady the Screen pointer on the **UP ↑** arrow and **hold down** the left mouse button. *You should see the worksheet scrolling continuously downwards.*

FRAME 2.5

How to scroll a worksheet LEFT or RIGHT   ▼ ▲

❶ Steady the tip of the pointer on the **RIGHT →** arrow button of the **Horizontal scroll bar** (Fig.2.4) then click the left mouse button once. *The worksheet scrolls to the left revealing the next column.*

❷ Click on the **RIGHT →** arrow again. *The worksheet moves left revealing one more column.*

❸ Keep the pointer on the **RIGHT →** arrow and **hold down** the left mouse button. *You should see the worksheet scrolling continuously to the left revealing more columns.*

❹ Steady the pointer on the **LEFT ←** arrow and **hold down** the left mouse button. *The worksheet scrolls continuously to the right.*

HELP

You can move faster up and down, or left and right by **dragging** the **Fast Scroll box** (see Fig.2.4) to a different position on the **Scroll bar**. Also by clicking on the Scroll bar between the Fast Scroll box and an arrow you can move over a large interval of columns or rows.

INFO

Selecting cells

Before you can enter and manipulate data (information) in a worksheet you need to first select or 'highlight' the cell or cells you want to work with. Selecting cells is an essential first step in many operations. Being able to select groups of cells accurately requires a little practice. When a cell is selected it has a solid heavy rectangular border. In Figure 2.5, cell A1 is currently selected and is therefore the active cell. You can make three kinds of selections:

- single cell (Fig. 2.5)
- multiple cells (Fig. 2.6)
- non-adjacent selections (Fig. 2.7)

When a cell is selected it is 'active'. In Figure 2.6, although a range of cells have been selected only cell B2 is active at present. Similarly, in Figure 2.7, only cell F7 is presently active. Whenever data is typed it will appear in whichever cell is active at the time.

HELP

When selecting a range of cells, you may drag your Screen pointer too far over unwanted cells. Don't panic. Pull the pointer inwards or upwards as the case may be until you get the right range of cells then let go of the mouse button.

DO Exercise 2.5 - and practise selecting and highlighting cells.

Figure 2.5 Single cell selection

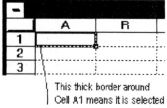

This thick border around
Cell A1 means it is selected

Figure 2.6 Multiple cell selection

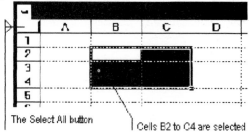

The Select All button

Cells B2 to C4 are selected

Figure 2.7 Non-adjacent cells selection

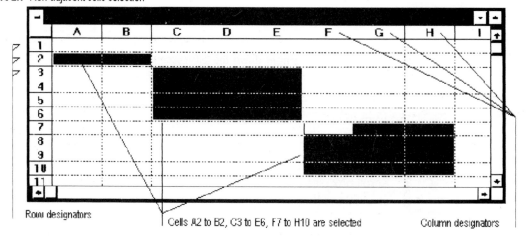

Row designators

Cells A2 to B2, C3 to E6, F7 to H10 are selected

Column designators

[a] Using the information given below, practise **selecting** and **deselecting** (1)

FRAME 2.6

How to **SELECT** a **SINGLE** cell eg, cell A5

Steady the Screen pointer inside the cell (eg, **A5**) and click the left mouse button once. *When correctly executed, a solid rectangular border will surround the cell indicating that it is active ie, ready to receive data.*

How to **SELECT MULTIPLE** cells eg, cell B2 to C4 (see Fig. 2.6)

to cell **C2** and down to cell **C4**, then release the mouse button. *When correctly executed, the selected range of cells will be surrounded by a dark rectangle. The 'active' cell in the range ie, B2, will remain white.*

FRAME 2.8

How to **DESELECT** a cell or a range of cells

Steady the Screen pointer inside any cell and click the left mouse button.

Remember

1. Inside a cell, the **Screen pointer** looks like this:

FRAME 2.9

How to select **NON-ADJACENT** cells eg, cells A2 to B2, C3 to E6 and F7 to H10 (see Fig. 2.7)

❶**Hold down** the CTRL key.

(NOTE: **Unless** you have made a mistake and want to start again, you should not release this key during the following stages, until you are told to do so).

Now:

∇ **select** and **drag** cell **A2** across to cell **B2**, then let go of the mouse button only and;

∇ **select** and **drag** cell **C3** across to cell **E3** and down to cell **E6**, then let go of the mouse button and;

∇ **select** and **drag** cell **F7** across to cell **H7** and down to cell **H10**, then let go of the mouse button.

❷**Release** the CTRL key. *Your cells selection should now look like Figure 2.7. If not, deselect and try again*

2. In order to **drag**, position the Screen pointer on the cell, then press the left mouse tbutton and hold it down while moving the mouse.

FRAME 2.10

How to select a **ROW** or **COLUMN** eg, row 1 or column A

Steady the Screen pointer on the **Row-designator** (eg, row **1**) or **Column-designator** (eg, column **A)** and click the left mouse button. *The entire row or column should appear on a dark background indicating that it has been selected.*

FRAME 2.11

How to select **MULTIPLE ROWS** or **COLUMNS**

Steady the Screen pointer on the **Row or Column-designator** you want to start with, and **drag** to the Row or Column-designator you want to finish with, then release the mouse button. *The range of rows or columns will be highlighted.*

FRAME 2.12

How to select **ALL CELLS** in a worksheet

Steady the Screen pointer on the **Select All** button (See Fig. 2.6) and click the left mouse button. *The entire worksheet should be highlighted.*

Entering data in a spreadsheet

Text, numbers, formulae, dates and times can be stored in cells. Now that you are reasonably familiar with the Excel worksheet let's create a worksheet.

Please note that what you type will initially appear in the 'active' cell and in the **Formula area** (see Fig. 2.8). When you press the ENTER key or click the left button on your mouse, the data will be transferred to the chosen cell. It follows that, for the data to be transferred to the right cell you must have chosen/selected the desired cell in the first place, before starting to type your data.

OVERVIEW OF THE STEPS FOR ENTERING DATA

Select the cell you want your data to appear in. (For help, refer to FRAME 2.6, p33);

Use the keyboard to type your data; (remember what you type at this stage will appear in the **Formula area** and in the **active** cell.

Read and **Correct** any noticeable errors using the BACKSPACE and **Delete** keys (see Table 2, p6) as you would if you were word processing.

Transfer the data from the Formula area to the chosen cell by doing one of the following:
- press the RIGHT arrow key to move to the next column or
- press the DOWN arrow key to move to the next row or
- click the 'tick' box that appears next to the **Formula area** or
- move and steady the **Screen pointer** on the next required cell and click the left mouse button.

When entering data in the worksheet you may find it more convenient to use a combination of the ARROW keys on the keyboard and the mouse.

DO Exercise 2.6 - and practise entering and editing data in Excel worksheet.

Figure 2.8 An Excel worksheet containing data

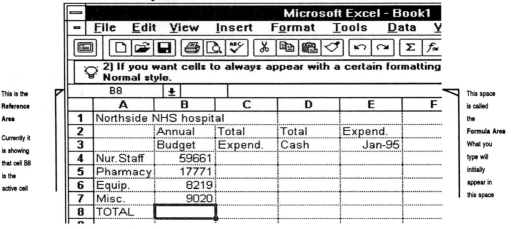

merge to contain the data. Now, enter the rest
Figure 2.8. Make sure that your cells coincide with that of Figure 2.8. When you've finished please go on to the next page.

FRAME 2.13

 How to enter data and correct typing errors

❶ **Select** cell **A2** then type any letter of the alphabet. *The letter you have typed should appear in the Formula area with an I-beam cursor flashing after it.*

Press the BACKSPACE on the keyboard once. *The character is erased.*
Pressing the BACKSPACE always erases characters in a reverse direction just as if you were using a word processor.

Select cell **B4** and type any five letter word, then press the RIGHT arrow key once. *This removes the word you've typed in the Formula area and transfers it into cell B4.*

Select cell **B4**, then press the SPACEBAR once.
The character is erased. This is only one way of erasing wrong entries in any cell. Later on you will find out other ways.

Remember

1. The **BACKSPACE** key on the keyboard is on the top row next to the PLUS sign

2. The **RIGHT arrow** key is one of the four arrows on your keyboard.
↑
←↓→
These keys can be used to move from one cell to another in all four directions.

HELP

- If you make a typing mistake, press the BACKSPACE key to erase and then retype.
- When the **Caps Lock** is OFF, everything you type will be written in lowercase and vice versa. To switch on the **Caps Lock** , press the **Caps Lock** key once. To switch it off again, press the **Caps Lock** key once again.
- When the **Caps Lock** is OFF, to type a character in UPPERcase simply hold down the SHIFT (⇧) key and press the letter you require and vice versa.
- As you start entering your data, you would notice that words are automatically aligned to the left of the cell, while figures (ie, values) are automatically aligned to the right of the cell. If you notice that some labels overlap into the next column, don't worry about these at this stage. Continue typing your data.
- The number **0** is next to the letter 9; the letter **O** is between the letters I and P
- After each entry, to transfer the data from the Formula area to the cell you will need to press one of the keys mentioned in item 4 on page 34.

Inserting and deleting text

Contents of any cell can be changed and this section shows you how to do this. Before rushing to do the exercise, spend a moment reading the difference between an **Insertion point** and the **Screen pointer**, then read the overview which follows. Later on when you need a refresher on Inserting and deleting text, just reread the overview.

SCREEN POINTER v/s INSERTION POINT

- **The Screen pointer** is an icon that moves as you move the mouse. The shape of the Screen pointer changes as it is moved to different parts of the Excel worksheet (*see* Table 1, p5).
- **The Insertion point** is an icon that shows where the next character you type will appear in the working area. The Insertion point is sometimes referred to as the Cursor, and is always a blinking vertical line (|). In the Formula area of the worksheet, the Screen pointer looks like this: I.

OVERVIEW ON EDITING TEXT

Characters, words, sentences, numbers and formulae in a cell can be replaced by overtyping over existing entries or by editing part of the cell entry. If you need to edit only part of the cell entry, the data needs to be transferred back to the **Formula area** before such corrections can be made.

Editing text in the Formula area

Select the cell containing the data. *Its contents will appear in the Formula area. (N.B. For data which spread over several cells eg, a sentence; you need to select the first cell where the sentence originates).*

Steady the I-beam pointer in the desired location and click the left mouse button. *The Insertion point will immediately move to that spot and start to flash.*

(To delete text) **Press** the **Delete** key to erase text to the right of the Insertion point and press the BACKSPACE key to erase text to the left of the Insertion point.

(To Insert text) **Type** your text and it will be inserted where the Insertion point is.

Editing contents of a cell by overtyping

Select the cell containing the data. *Its contents will appear in the Formula area.*

Start typing *and all cell contents will be overwritten. There is no need to move the Screen pointer into the Formula area or to delete the text first.*

 DO Exercise 2.7 - it will lead you step-by-step through making changes using the data you typed in **Practice box 3** on the previous page. Please ensure the document on your screen looks like that in Figure 2.8, p34.

Using the information on the left page and in FRAME | **Remember**

3   Insert the word **left** after the word ~~such~~

4   Replace the word **TOTAL** with **Yr.TOTAL** in cell A8.

5   Change the figures **8219** in cell B6 to **3285**.

6   Overwrite the figures **3285** in cell B6 with **8219**.

keys on the keyboard

↑
←↓→

FRAME 2.14

To **insert** a character at the beginning of a word eg, take→**s**take	❶ Select the desired cell Position the Insertion point immediately before the letter **t** and click the left mouse button. Type **s**, then press ENTER.	To **delete** a character at the beginning of a word eg, **s**take→ take	❶ Select the desired cell Position the Insertion point immediately before the letter **t** and click the left mouse button. Press BACKSPACE
To **insert** a character in a word. eg, wet→w**h**et	❶ Select the desired cell Position the Insertion point after the letter **w** and click the left mouse button. Type **h**, then press **ENTER**.	To **delete** a character in a word. eg, w**h**et→wet	❶ Select the desired cell Position the Insertion point after the letter **w** and click the left mouse button. Press DELETE
To **insert** a character at the end of a word eg, take→take**n**	❶ Select the desired cell Position the Insertion point immediately after the letter **e** and click the left mouse button. Type **n**, then press ENTER.	To **delete** a character at the end of a word eg, take→take**n**	❶ Select the desired cell Position the Insertion point immediately after the letter **e** and click the left mouse button. Press DELETE
To **insert** a **word** in a sentence eg, Excel is a spreadsheet → Excel is a **flexible** spreadsheet.	❶ Select the desired cell Position the Insertion point immediately before the letter **s** of the word **spreadsheet** and click the left mouse button. Type **flexible** and press SPACEBAR, then press ENTER.	To **delete** a **word** in a sentence eg, Excel is a **flexible** spreadsheet →Excel is a spreadsheet.	❶ Select the desired cell Position the Insertion point immediately before the letter **f** of the word **flexible** and click the left mouse button. Press DELETE.
To **insert** a **word** at the end of a sentence	❶ Select the desired cell Position the Insertion point immediately after the last letter and click the left mouse button. Press SPACEBAR and type your word, then press ENTER.	To **delete** a **word** at the end of a sentence	❶ Select the desired cell Position the Insertion point immediately before the first letter of the word and click the left mouse button. Press DELETE

As long as your computer remains switched on and the machine does not fail, your worksheet will stay in the computer random access memory (RAM). Once the computer is switched off or your PC crashes, your document will be lost for ever. Although we are finished with this worksheet for now, you will need it for future lessons. To save this worksheet permanently, you can store it on a disk. In this workbook you will be required to save the worksheet on a floppy disk in drive A, not on the computer's hard disk (drive C) or the computer's network hard disk (drive N).

Take a look at your screen, focus on the **Title bar**. You should be able to see that your document has no name. It is simply shown as Sheet1. This is because it is a new worksheet. To give it a name you must save it to disk. There are two commands you can use to save your new document. The **Save As** and **Save** commands.

- **Save As** command is used to save a worksheet for the first time or to rename a document.
- **Save** command is used to save changes made to an existing worksheet. This command saves your worksheet under the same name with which it was last saved, thus replacing the previous version.

All new worksheet must have a unique name which can be no more than eight characters long. The name may be a mixture of letters and numbers with <u>no</u> <u>spaces</u> in between characters. As our worksheet is new we will need to use the **Save As** command so that we can give it a name. For our purpose I suggest you save the document to a **floppy disk** and call it: **MYTASK1**

DO Exercise 2.8 - and learn how to save your new unnamed worksheet to disk.

Figure 2.10

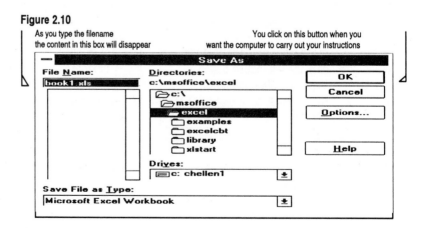

As you type the filename the content in this box will disappear

You click on this button when you want the computer to carry out your instructions

...listed in FRAME 2.15 **below**, save your worksheet as

❶ Insert an appropriately formatted floppy disk into drive A.

Point to the **disk** icon, located on the **Standard Toolbar** and click the left mouse button. *A 'Save As' dialog box should appear with the cursor flashing in a little box labelled File Name.*

Ignore anything you see in the File Name box and Type the drive letter (including the colon) **a:**
As you start typing, anything present in the File Name box will be overwritten.

Leaving no spaces between characters, type the **Filename**.

Point to the command **OK** and click the left mouse button (or press the ENTER key). If another dialog box appears, click on **OK**. *Provided everything is correct, after a few seconds the worksheet will be saved to your floppy disk, and Excel will retain the worksheet on the screen allowing you to continue working on it if you wish.*
NOTE: *If you now look on the Title bar you should see the name of your worksheet. The .XLS means that this is an Excel file.*

good care of your floppy disk, your floppy disk will take care of your data.

2. The extension XLS is automatically added by the program.

3. An error message will appear if you type the wrong instructions, such as putting a semi-colon instead of a colon. Click on OK and do Steps 4 and 5 again.

ATTENTION   **We have come to the end of this lesson**. Please, close down Excel, then shut down Windows following the steps listed in FRAMES 1.10 and 1.11. However, if you would like to continue straight away with the next lesson, you **must** close down Excel now, and then restart it again.

Warning

- Never switch off the computer before you have saved all your work to disk. Otherwise, everything that was in the computer's Random Access Memory (RAM) will be lost. (Read **HELP** box below.)
- Always remove your floppy disk from the drive before switching off the machine.

HELP

We have now saved the worksheet on to a floppy disk in **drive A**. As suggested you called it **MYTASK1**. Do not forget that you will need it for future lessons. So keep the disk in a safe place and make sure you do not inadvertently erase or overwrite this file. If you wanted to save MYTASK1 to any other drive (eg, **drive B**, **drive C**, **drive N**), this is the procedure:

- To save MYTASK1 to the hard disk drive C or N, at Step 3 you simply type: **MYTASK1**
- To save MYTASK1 to a floppy disk in drive B, then at Step 3 you simply type: **B:MYTASK1**

1   When Excel is loaded, a blank worksheet appears on the screen. In Excel version 4.0 the worksheet is called **Sheet1** and in version 5.0 it is called **book1**. The system is ready for you to enter your data.

2   The new worksheet is unnamed and has a total of 255 columns across, and 16,384 rows down (255 x 16,384 = 4,177,920 cells in total). The VDU is not big enough to show all the rows and columns. At best you are likely to see 20 rows and 9 columns at a time.

3   You enter data in Excel using the keyboard in the same manner as you would if you were using a word processor.

4   To correct errors during typing, you use the BACKSPACE (←) button on the keyboard which is next to the plus (+) sign.

5   To delete text using a combination of keyboard and mouse, you place the **Insertion point** immediately after the text to be deleted, then press the BACKSPACE button - once for each character to be deleted.

6   The contents of any cell cannot be edited directly. To insert text, you place the **Insertion point** between the appropriate letters or words in the Formula area, then type the missing letter or words.

7   To leave a space between words you press the SPACEBAR, just as you would when using a word processor.

8   A new worksheet does not have a name. Before it can be saved to disk, it needs to be given a unique name which should not be more than eight characters long. This name can be a mixture of letters and numbers but it must have no spaces in between characters. Excel will automatically put an **.XLS** extension to worksheets saved to disk.

9   To avoid loss of work due to power failure, it is good practice to save work in progress regularly.

10   To save work to a floppy disk in **drive A**, you need to state the drive letter followed by the filename eg, **A:MYTASK1**

Before we close down this lesson remember these two points:

Warning

- The Excel window has some features which are similar to other windows. The procedures for using these features are the same.
- If you attempt to save your work to a disk which has not been properly formatted, Excel will refuse to obey your command and an error message may appear. Similarly, if your disk is damaged, you will not be able to save anything on it. More importantly, you will not be able to retrieve work saved on it.

saved the file called ... when you completed lesson 2. Do not save it in

computer memory until you are instructed to do so. Simply.

- switch on the computer and monitor now and load Windows 3.1*
- start Excel for Windows*
- before starting any of the ensuing exercises, ensure your Sheet window and the Microsoft Excel window are merged into one (refer to page 26 Fig. 2.1 and 2.2)

*Refer to FRAMES 1.1 and 2.1 as necessary.

	At the end of this lesson you should be able to: ▼ ▲
EXERCISE3.1	1 identify the cell border and Fill-handle; 2 recognize data series; 3 move data from cell to cell and create data series using the drag and drop technique.
EXERCISE3.2	4 identify the correct commands to edit a worksheet; 5 use the Delete and Clear commands appropriately and skilfully.
EXERCISE3.3	6 identify the following edit commands; **Cut**, **Copy** and **Paste**; 7 use the above edit commands appropriately and skilfully.
EXERCISE3.4	8 understand the concept of saving, retrieving, and renaming a document; 9 retrieve and rename a document from a floppy disk;
EXERCISE3.5	10 identify the row designators (headings); 11 insert and delete rows in a worksheet as required;
EXERCISE3.6	12 identify the column designators (headings); 13 insert and delete columns in a worksheet as required;
EXERCISE3.8	14 understand the concept of naming and renaming a document; 15 save a named worksheet under a new name;
EXERCISE3.8	16 recognize the double headed arrow used for adjusting column widths; 17 adjust column widths.

Using the drag technique to input and move data

In the previous lesson we saved a worksheet to a floppy disk. We named it **mytask1**. Later on in this lesson and subsequent ones, we are going to use this worksheet and add more and more information to it. Then after each lesson we are going to save our worksheet under a new name. Before we start further work on our last worksheet please read on and then do the suggested exercises.

Figure 3.1

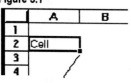

The **Fill handle**

Creating data series

When creating a worksheet, you can speed up some types of data entry by making skilful use of the **Fill handle** (ie, the small solid square located on the lower-right corner of the rectangular border which surrounds the selected cell or cells, see Fig. 3.1) to extend serial data such as 1,2,3 to include 4,5,6 ... Further examples of serial data are listed in Table 3.1 on the left. Being able to create a **data series** is a very useful and a fairly easy technique to master.

Table 3.1 Series of data relating to Time

By dragging the **Fill-handle** the following types of data can be entered:			
from one or two cells		**to** multiple cells	
8:00	9:00	10:00	11:00
Mon	Tue	Wed	Thu
Jan	Feb	Mar	Apr
22-Jan	23-Jan	24-Jan	25-Jan
Jan-95	Feb-95	Mar-95	Apr-95
Jan-95	Apr-95	Jul-95	Oct-95	Jan-96
22-Jan	22-Apr	22-Jul	22-Oct	22-Jan
1995	1996	1997	1998	1999

Table 3.2 Series of Linear data

By dragging the **Fill-handle** the following types of data can be entered:			
from one or two cells		**to** multiple cells	
1	2	3	4	5
1	3	5	7	9
50	45	40	35	30

Here are two types of series that can be created in Excel:

- **Time**. A time series can include increments of days, weeks or months that you specify, or repeating sequences such as weekdays, month names, or quarters (see examples in Table 3.1.)
- **Linear** When you create a linear series, Excel increases or decreases values by a constant value, (see examples in Table 3.2.)

Moving data

Occasionally you may have typed data in the wrong cell. You can easily move this data by using a technique called **drag and drop**. This involves dragging the thick rectangular border surrounding the selected cell or cells. To use this method you will need to place the pointer against the said rectangular border. When positioned correctly the pointer will take the shape of an arrow leaning to the left (see Figure 3.2 below).

Figure 3.2 - Showing where to place the Screen pointer before moving cell by dragging.

DO Exercise 3.1 - and practise moving data from cell to cell and creating series.

...Type Jan-95 in cell **C5** and press the RIGHT arrow key. *Notice how Excel*

---

❶ **Select** the cell containing the data you want to move;

❷ **Steady** the Screen pointer anywhere **on** the **thick rectangular border** framing the cell. *When the pointer is correctly positioned, its shape changes to an arrow leaning to the left.*

❸ **Drag** the rectangular frame to the new location, then release the mouse button.

N.B. You should only drag while the pointer is shaped as an arrow leaning to the left.

When properly executed, the content of the cell will move to the new location. If not, select the cell, then try again.

Screen pointer looks like when it is leaning to the left.

2. To **drag** you press the left mouse button and hold it down while moving the mouse.

 EXERCISE 3.1

[c] Ensure cell **A2** contains the data **Jan-95**.

[d] Using the 4-steps **below**, extend the contents of cell **A2** to cell **D2**.

[e] Using the 3-steps **above**, move the data series in cells **A2-D2** to a different location of your choice.

[f] Experiment creating a few series of your own, but include the following: **Mon**, **Group 1**, **23rd March**, then try moving each range of cells containing a series to different locations.

FRAME 3.2

| ☐ | **How to create a series by dragging the Fill-handle** | |

❶ **Select** the cell or cells containing the data. *A thick rectangular border should surround it.*

❷ **Steady** the Screen pointer on the **Fill-handle** (see Fig. 3.1). *When the pointer is correctly positioned its shape changes to a plus sign.*

❸ **Drag** the **Fill-handle** over the range of cells you want the data to appear, then release the mouse button.

N.B. You should only drag while the pointer is shaped as a a plus sign shown in the right-margin.

❹ **Remove** the highlight. *When properly executed, the chosen range of cells should contain a data series. If not, select the cell, then try again.*

Remember

3. This is how the **Screen pointer** looks like when it changes to a plus sign

4. If you drag a series over unwanted cells, keep holding the mouse button down and drag back.

Using editing commands to remove the contents of cell(s)

Whenever you need to remove data from Excel worksheet you can use the **Clear** or **Delete** command. Clearing a cell or cells removes the contents, formats, or notes - or all three - from the cell(s), but leaves the cleared cell(s) in the structure of the worksheet; while deleting a cell or cells completely removes the cell(s) from the worksheet, and moves adjacent cells to close up the space that was occupied by the deleted cell or cells.

Warning

The Clear and Delete commands should be used with caution especially when cells being cleared or deleted contain formulae. However, if you inadvertently delete or clear cells by mistake, you can restore them by choosing the **Undo** command from the **Edit** menu <u>before</u> doing anything else on your worksheet.

If you have just completed Exercise 3.1 you should have on your screen a worksheet containing some data. As we do not require these anymore, they can be removed from the worksheet thus freeing computer memory.

N.B. - In some of the ensuing exercises you will be asked to use the RIGHT mouse button as well as the left. Do make sure you press the correct button as instructed.

 DO Exercise 3.2 - and practise using the **Clear** and **Delete** command to erase unwanted data. After completing this exercise I suggest you switch off your computer and take a short break before continuing.

Using the steps in the appropriate box below,

Remember

[d] Erase the entire worksheet using the command **Delete**

FRAME 3.3

 How to use the command Delete

❶ Steady the Screen pointer on a cell containing data and click the **RIGHT** mouse button. *A thick border surrounds the chosen cell and a command list appears.*

❷ Steady the Screen pointer on the command **Delete** and click the left mouse button (or press the letter **D**). *A 'Delete' dialog box appears.*

❸ **Point** to the white spot next to **Shift Cells Left** or **Shift Cells Up**, and click the left mouse button (or press the letter **L** or **U**). *A black dot appears inside the white spot to acknowledge your chosen option..*

❹ **Point** to the command **OK** and click the left mouse button (or press ENTER). *The cell and its contents disappears from the worksheet.*

FRAME 3.4

How to use the command Clear

❶ Steady the Screen pointer on a cell containing data and click the **RIGHT** mouse button. *A thick border surrounds the chosen cell and a command list appears.*

❷ **For Excel version 4.0:**
(a) Steady the Screen pointer on the command **Clear** and click the left mouse button. *A 'Clear' dialog box appears.*
(b) **Point** to the white spot next to the option **All** (or press the letter **A**). *A black dot appears inside the white spot to acknowledge your chosen option.*
(c) **Point** to the command **OK** and click the left mouse button. *The contents of the cell disappears.*

For Excel version 5.0:
Steady the Screen pointer on the command **Clear contents** and click the left mouse button.

FRAME 3.5

How to remove the contents of an entire worksheet using the command Clear ▼ ▲

❶ Steady the Screen pointer on the **Select All button** (see Fig. 2.6, p32) and click the **RIGHT** mouse button. *A command list should appear on a darkened worksheet.*

❷ **For Excel version 4.0:**
(a) **Point** and click on the command **Clear**. *A 'Clear' dialog box should appear.*
(b) **Point** to the white spot next to option **All** and click the left mouse button (or press **A**). *A black dot should appear inside the white spot to acknowledge your chosen option.*
(c) **Point** and click on the command **OK** (or press ENTER), then remove the highlight.
All contents in the worksheet will be erased leaving a clear screen.

For Excel version 5.0:
Point and click on the command **Clear contents.**

FRAME 3.6

How to erase an entire worksheet using the command Delete

❶ Steady the Screen pointer on the **Select All button** (see Fig. 2.6, p32) and click the **RIGHT** mouse button. *A command list should appear on a darkened worksheet.*

❷ **Point** and click on the command **Delete**. *All contents in the worksheet will be erased leaving a dark screen.*

 **INFO**

Using other editing commands to input or move data

When you have entered data in the wrong cells, you can use the technique 'drag and drop', as discussed previously, to transfer the data to the correct cell or cells. You can also use the **Cut and Paste** commands to achieve the same purpose. Furthermore, using the 'Fill handle' you can copy data to adjacent cells, by using the **Copy and Paste** commands you can copy data to non-adjacent cells or to another worksheet altogether.

Both cut and paste or copy and paste involve selecting one or more cells, and then copying them to another part of the worksheet. Cutting cells, physically removes them from their original location so that they can be pasted to a new location while copying cells simply copies the data to a new location without interfering with the original cells or data.

When you cut or copy cells, Excel stores them in a temporary memory called the Clipboard. They stay there until they are replaced by some other edit command.

DO Exercise 3.3 - and practise using the **Cut, Copy and Paste** commands to move data from one location to another.

Figure 3.3 Example of a command list when you click the RIGHT mouse button.

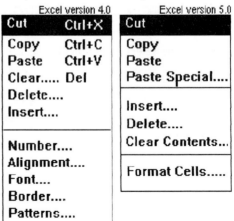

[a] Type the following data in your worksheet.

data from cell A1 and put it in cell D1.

[c] Using the commands **Copy** and **Paste**, copy the data in cell A2 into cell D2.

[d] Using the information given in FRAMES 3.9 and 3.8 below, copy the contents of cells B1-C1 into cell C4.

 [*Notice how Excel automatically copies the data into cells C4 and D4*].

[e] Practise copying other range of cells.

[f] Select the entire worksheet (refer to FRAME 3.6, p45 for help) and delete all the contents of the worksheet, then move on.

FRAME 3.7

How to move data using the commands Cut and Paste

❶ Steady the Screen pointer on the required cell (eg, cell A1) and click the **RIGHT** mouse button.
A thick rectangular border surrounds the cell and a command list should also appear.

❷ **Point** to the command **Cut** and click the left mouse button. *A marquee should surround the cell.*

❸ Steady the Screen pointer on the cell you want to paste in the data (eg, cell D1) and click the **RIGHT** mouse button.
A thick rectangular border surrounds the cell and a command list should also appear.

❹ **Point** to the command **Paste** and click the left mouse button. *The data from the cell you selected in Step 1 should move to the cell you selected in Step 3.*

FRAME 3.8

How to copy data using the commands Copy and Paste

❶ Steady the Screen pointer on the required cell (eg, cell A2) and click the **RIGHT** mouse button.
A thick rectangular border surrounds the cell and a command list should also appear.

❷ **Point** to the command **Copy** and click the left mouse button. *A marquee should surround the cell.*

❸ Steady the Screen pointer on the cell you want to copy in the data (eg, cell D2) and click the **RIGHT** mouse button.
A thick rectangular border surrounds the cell and a command list should also appear.

❹ **Point** to the command **Paste** and click the left mouse button. *The data from the cell you selected in Step 1 should move to the cell you selected in Step 3.*

❺ Press ESCape key to remove the marquee which surrounds the cell you were copying the data from.

FRAME 3.9

How to select a range of cell and the shortcut menu

Select the range of cells (refer to p33, for help), then place the Screen pointer in the first cell of the range and click the **RIGHT** mouse button.

 # Retrieving and renaming a document

From the previous exercise, you should have a clear screen. Before I ask you to load into the computer memory the worksheet - **MYTASK1** - which you saved onto a floppy disk in the last lesson, so that we can work on it again, read and note the following.

Retrieving
- Loading a worksheet from disk to the computer memory is called **Retrieving**, **Reading** or **Opening**. Before you can do this, the relevant disk must be in the disk drive.
- If you know the filename and the drive(as we do), then you simply type them in the **File Name** box (Fig. 3.4) and click the **OK** button. The file will load and appear on the screen, provided you have not made a spelling error or used the wrong disk.
- To retrieve a file which name you have forgotten, you could look at the **File list**. From the **File list** you could select the file by pointing to it and clicking the left mouse button. The selected file should then appear in the **File Name** box. For files on drive A, the drive letter may need to be changed (see Fig. 3.4).
- To retrieve a file from disk, you can use the **Open** command on the File menu bar or you can select the **Open File** icon. If the document was one of the last four Microsoft Excel documents used, you can also retrieve it by choosing the document name from the bottom of the Extend list, which should appear once you have selected open **File**

Renaming
- When reading, for example, the file **MYTASK1** from the floppy disk, all that is effectively happening is that an image copy of that document is being read into the computer memory (RAM). A copy of **MYTASK1** will still remain on the disk. If you make amendments to that copy you have in the computer memory, and then use the **Save** command or click on the **Save** Icon to save a copy to disk, the amended version will overwrite the previous version. If you want to preserve the previous version (as we do), you will need to rename the document ie, give it a different name.

 DO Exercise 3.4 - it will help you **retrieve** and **rename** the worksheet **MYTASK1** from your floppy disk. I suggest we rename it as, **MYTASK2**.

Figure 3.4 Dialog box for opening a document

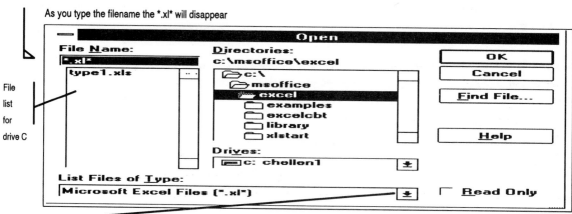

As you type the filename the *.xl* will disappear

File list for drive C

To change to another drive point to this arrow and click the left mouse button.
You may need to scroll up to find the drive letter you require. To select, click the drive letter.

...ing to add more information to the worksheet MYTASK1 which

FRAME 3.10

 How to retrieve a file from a floppy disk in drive A

❶ **Insert** the floppy disk containing the required file(s) in drive **A**.

❷ **Point** to the File icon on the **Standard Toolbar** and click the left mouse button. *An 'Open' dialog box (Fig.3.4) should appear with *.xl* highlighted in the small box under file name.*

❸ Ignore anything you may see in the **File Name** box and type the drive letter **a:** *As you start typing anything present in the File name box will be overwritten.*

❹ Leaving no spaces between any characters, type the **Filename.**

❺ **Point** to the command **OK** and click the left mouse button (or press the ENTER key). **N.B If a dialog box should appear asking you if you want to update, point to the command YES and click the left mouse button.** *The light on drive A should engage. Provided everything is correct, after a few seconds the file you requested should appear on the screen.*

FRAME 3.11

 How to rename a file on a floppy disk in drive A

❶ Ensure your floppy disk is in drive **A**.

❷ **Point** to the word **File** on the **Menu bar** and click the left mouse button (or **hold down** the ALT key and press **F**). *An extended list of commands should appear.*

❸ **Point** and click on the **Save As** (or press the letter **A**). *A 'Save As' dialog box should appear with a suggested name highlighted in the File **Name** box.*

❹ Ignore what is in the **File Name** box and type the drive letter **a:** *As you start typing the previous name will be overwritten.*

❺ Leaving no spaces between any characters, type the new **Filename**.

❻ **Point** to the command **OK** and click the left mouse button (or press the ENTER (↵) key). *Provided everything is correct, after a few seconds the worksheet will be saved to the floppy disk under the new name you entered. Excel will retain the worksheet on the screen so that you can work on it.* **NOTE:** *If you now look on the **Title bar**, you should see the title now bears the new name.*

Inserting and deleting rows or columns

As a reminder, we presently have two copies of the same worksheet on disk. One is called **MYTASK1** and the other, **MYTASK2**. We also have a copy of 'mytask2' still in the computer memory. Please, read the **HELP** box below to see what you should do if you inadvertently spoil your worksheet during the ensuing exercises.

Once you have entered data on a worksheet, it is sometimes necessary to insert blank cells between occupied cells to make room for new data or to include more white space in the data area. You can insert entire blank rows or columns anywhere on the worksheet. When you insert cells, Excel shifts the other cells in your worksheet to make room for the inserted cells and adjusts references to the shifted cells to reflect their new locations.

You may equally want to delete unwanted cells which may or may not contain data. When deleting a row or column of cells Excel will remove the cells and any data they may contain from the worksheet, and move adjacent cells to close up the space that was occupied by the deleted cells. If you are ready let's try the next exercise.

DO Exercise 3.5 - it will give you practice in inserting and deleting rows of cells.

Figure 3.5 Showing the Row and Column-designators(headings), and the Fill handle

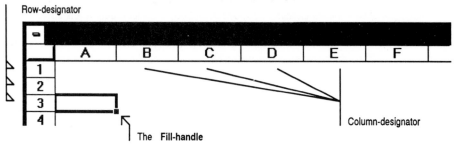

Since **MYTASK2** is a renamed copy of **MYTASK1**, until we make alterations to it, the contents and format will remain the same. If during the ensuing exercises you inadvertently spoil your worksheet, do not panic but do the following:

1 Try using the **Undo** command immediately to remedy the situation.

2 However, if this does not work, simply reload a fresh copy from your floppy (refer to Table 3.3). Of course, in such a situation, any alterations you would have made in this lesson, would need to be done again to make the worksheet look like Figure 3.6 at the end of this lesson.

Table 3.3

The following steps should help you to reload a fresh copy of a fille eg, **MYTASK2.XLS**

1. Hold down **ALT** key and press **F**
2. Press **C**
3. Press **N**
4. Hold down **ALT** key and press **F**
5. You should now be able to see the names of up to 4 files listed at the bottom of the **Extended menu**.

One of them should be the name of the file you want. Click on this file or press the number in front of it.

Using the information given below in FRAMES 3.12 and 3.13, carry out

How to remove a row from a worksheet

❶ Steady the Screen pointer on the **Row-designator** (see Fig. 3.5, p50) and click the **RIGHT** mouse button. *The selected row will appear on a dark background and a command list should also appear.*

❷ Steady the Screen pointer on the command **Delete**, then click the left mouse button (or press **D)**. *The row including its contents should vanish. Excel will also shifted up the rows in the worksheet to fill the space.*

1. To undo an action , **Hold down** CTRL and press the letter Z. or click on **Edit** then click on **Undo**.

FRAME 3.13

How to insert a blank row in a worksheet

NOTE: To insert a blank row between two existing rows such as rows 1 and 2, you'll need to select the **Row-designator** for the second row ie, **Row-designator 2**.

❶ Steady the Screen pointer on the appropriate **Row-designator** (see Fig.3.5), and click the **RIGHT** mouse button. *The entire row will highlight and a command list should appear*

❷ Steady the Screen pointer on the command **Insert**, then click the left mouse button (or press the letter **I)**. *A new blank row should appear between the two existing rows.*

❸ Steady the Screen pointer in an empty cell and click the left mouse button. *This removes the highlight. You should now be able to see the new row clearly.*

Remember

2. If you **select** a cell by clicking on the RIGHT mouse button , a shortcut menu will also appear.

 EXERCISE 3.5

[d] Now let's add some more data to your worksheet:
1 Select cell **A2**, then type **Princess Diana Unit**;
2 Select the **row-designator** labelled **3** and insert a blank row;
3 Select cell **A3**, then type **Expenditure for the 1st quarter 1995**;
4 Select cell **E4** and extend its contents to cell **H4** by dragging the **Fill-handle** (see Fig 3.5 and refer to p43 for help on creating data series).
5 Select cell **E5** and extend its contents to cell **H5**;
[e] Select a blank cell to remove the highlight, then move on.

In the previous exercise you learned how to insert and delete rows in a worksheet. You also added fresh data to your worksheet. Your worksheet should now be similar in content to that of Figure 3.6. If not please make the necessary adjustments before continuing.

Warning

You should always use caution when deleting cells. Deleting cells that contain formulae referring to them might produce erroneous calculations. However, if you inadvertently delete cells you want to keep, you can restore them by immediately by holding down the CTRL key and pressing the letter Z, or by choosing the **Undo** command from the **Edit** menu **before** doing anything else on your worksheet.

The steps for inserting and deleting columns are very similar to that of rows.

DO Exercise 3.6 - it will give you practice in inserting and deleting columns.

Figure 3.6 Shows the contents of the worksheet after the last exercise.

	A	B	C	D	E	F	G	H	I	
1	Northside NHS Trust hospital									
2	Princess Diana Unit									
3	Expenditure for the 1st quarter 1995									
4		Annual	Total	Total	Expend.	Expend.	Expend.	Expend.		
5		Budget	Expend.	Cash left	Jan-95	Feb-95	Mar-95	Apr-95		
6	Nur.Staff	59661								
7	Pharmacy	17771								
8	Equip.	8219								
9	Misc.	9020								
10	Yr.TOTAL									
11										

[a] Using the information listed in FRAME 3.14 **insert** a **blank row** between the

NOTE: To insert a blank column between two existing columns, such as columns A and B, you'll need to select the second column ie, **Column-designator B**.

1 Steady the Screen pointer on the appropriate **column-designator** (see Fig. 3.5 p50), and click the **RIGHT** mouse button. *The entire column will highlight and a command list should appear.*

2 Steady the Screen pointer on the command **Insert**, then click the left mouse button (or press I). *A new blank column should appear.*

3 Steady the Screen pointer in an empty cell and click the left mouse button. *The highlight should disappear showing the new blank column.*

the wrong column , click on **Edit** then click on **Undo** or Hold down CTRL and press the letter Z.

 EXERCISE 3.6

[b] Using the steps listed in FRAME 3.15 **delete** the **blank** column **B** which you inserted in the above exercise, as this was only a trial. (*Clue: you'll need to select Column-designator B*).

[c] **Delete** column **H**.

FRAME 3.15

How to delete a column ▼ ▲

Remember

1 Steady the Screen pointer on the required **Column-designator** (see Fig. 3.5), and click the **RIGHT** mouse button. *The entire column will be highlighted and a command list should also appear.*

2 Steady the Screen pointer on the command **Delete**, then click the left mouse button (or press D). *The blank column should vanish and the gap closed.*

3 Steady the Screen pointer in an empty cell and click the left mouse button. *The highlight should disappear.*

First you select the appropriate column you want, then click the appropriate command. Excel will do the rest.

 EXERCISE 3.6

[d] Using the skills you have acquired so far, add the following text to the worksheet you currently have on your screen:

1 **Select** cell A12 and type: **PROJECTION**
2 **Select** cell A13 and type: **1st quart.**
3 **Select** cell A14 and type: **2nd quart.**
4 **Select** cell A15 and type: **3rd quart.**
5 **Select** cell A16 and type: **4th quart**
6 **Select** cell A17 and type: **Yr.TOTAL**

Saving a named document

Since you have been carrying out the exercises in this lesson, you have been making changes to **MYTASK2**, which is currently being temporarily stored in the computer's memory. Should you suddenly experience a power cut/failure, such as a fault in your electrical system, or you accidentally switch off the computer, all the changes you have made to this worksheet so far, would be lost.

As you will need this current worksheet for later use, I suggest you save it with the changes you have made this far. That way when you start the next lesson you can continue working on the worksheet. As pointed out before, there are two commands you can use to save a document. You have already used the command **Save As** in Exercises 2.8 and 3.4. As this is an existing document/worksheet , and we want to save it under its current name, we can use either the command **Save** from the **File menu** or the shortcut facility available on the **Toolbar**.

DO Exercise 3.7 - it will show you how to save this named-worksheet to your disk using both methods.

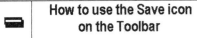
.... FRAME 3.16 or those in

FRAME 3.16

| | How to use the Save icon on the Toolbar | |

❶ Ensure your floppy disk is in drive **A**.

❷ Steady the Screen pointer on the **Save** icon located on the **Toolbar** and click the left mouse button. *The light on drive **A** should light up. Provided there is no error, a copy of the file with all the alterations would have been saved to your disk, and your document will remain on the screen. If you receive an error message, see* **HELP** *box below.*

FRAME 3.17

| | How to use the command Save from the File Menu | ▼ ▲ |

❶ Ensure your floppy disk is in drive **A**.

❷ Point to the command **File** on the **Menu bar** and click the left mouse button (or **hold down** the ALT key and press **F**).
An extended list of commands should appear.

❸ **Point** and click on the **Save** command (or press the letter **S**).
The light on drive A should light up. Provided there is no error, a copy of the file with all the alterations would have been saved to your disk, and your document will remain on the screen. If you receive an error message, see **HELP** *box below.*

| ? HELP | Sometimes you may experience difficulties saving your worksheet. There are several reasons for this. Here are some of them with possible solutions. If you are still unable to solve the problem, seek help from anyone available. |

• Your disk is faulty	• Buy reliable disks and take care of them.
• Your disk is write-protected or you have not inserted it in the drive properly.	• Remove the disk from the disk drive, take off the write-protection, if applicable and put the disk back into the drive.
• You have inserted the disk in the wrong disk drive	• Check that the disk is in the correct drive.

Changing column widths

Every time you call up a new worksheet, the width of all the columns are of the same size. You can increase or decrease the column width of selected columns as required. You can also have Excel adjust the column width for the **best fit** - ie, adjust the column width to fit the longest cell entry in a column.

Adjusting column width is important because whenever you enter a number that does not fit within the display boundary of the column width, Excel stores the data **but** displays these number signs (###) in the cell. In order to have the numbers fully displayed , you will need to increase the column width.

There are various ways of adjusting column widths. Before we try some of the methods, take a look at Figures 3.7 and 3.8 below.

- Notice the vertical lines which divide the letter headings.
- Notice also (Fig. 3.8) the **Double-headed arrow** with its own vertical line.

Whenever the Screen pointer is moved onto any one of these vertical lines it changes its shape into this double-headed arrow.

DO Exercise 3.8 - it will help you practise altering the width of columns in your worksheet.

Warning

After you have carried out the exercise on the next page, you will be asked to close down Excel and shut down Windows. You will most probably receive a message asking if you want to save the worksheet. **Do not** save the worksheet again. Click on the **NO** button.

Figure 3.7 Showing the vertical line which divides column designators/headings

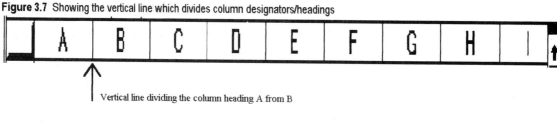

Vertical line dividing the column heading A from B

Figure 3.8 Showing the Double-headed arrowwith a vertical line between column headings A nd B

double-headed arrow with a vertical line resting on the
vertical line which divides the column heading A from B

Using the steps listed in Method 1 of FRAME 3.18 adjust the width of column A in

turn.

Remember to use the **Undo** facility to return the column(s) to its previous width before trying the next method.

simply **hold down** the CTRL key and press the letter **Z**

FRAME 3.18

How to adjust the width of a column or columns in a worksheet			
Method 1	**Method 2**	**Method 3**	**Method 4**
eg, to adjust the width of column A.	eg, to adjust the width of column A.	eg, to adjust the width of column A.	eg, to adjust the width of columns B to V
❶ Steady the Screen pointer on the **Column-designator** and click the left mouse button. *The whole column should highlight.* Steady the Screen pointer on the command **Format** on the **Menu bar** and click the left mouse button. *An command list should appear.* Point to the command **Column Width** or **Column** and click the left mouse button. **For Excel version 4.0** A **Column Width** dialog box should appear. You should now click on the command **Best fit.** **For Excel version 5.0** Another command list should appear. You should click on the command **Autofit Selection.** Remove the highlight (see FRAME 2.8, p33).	❶ Steady the pointer on the **Column-designator.** Gently move the Screen pointer and rest it on the verticle line that separates the **Column-designator A** from **B**. *As the Screen pointer rests on the verticle line its shape should change to a Double-headed arrow with a vertical line (see Fig.3.8).* **Drag** the vertical line to the right until its width is 13.50 or 13.57. The width is given in the **Reference area** (see Fig. 2.8, p38). *The width of column A should increase to accept the longest cell entry (which is the word projection cell A12).*	❶ Steady the Screen pointer on the appropriate **Column-designator** eg, Column-designator A. Gently move the Screen pointer and rest it on the verticle line that separates the **Column-designator A** from **B**. *As the Screen pointer rests on the verticle line its shape should change to a Double-headed arrow with a vertical line (see Fig.3.8).* Hold the **Double-headed arrow** pointer steady and double-click the left mouse button. *The width of column A should increase to accommodate the longest cell entry.*	❶ Steady the Screen pointer on the **Column-designator B** and **drag** across to **Column-designator V**, then release your mouse button. *Columns B to V should highlight to indicate that they are selected.* **Position** the Screen pointer on any of the selected cells, eg, **E12** and click the **RIGHT** mouse button. *A command list should appear.* Steady the pointer on the command **Column-Width** and click the left mouse button. *A Column Width Diaglog box should appear.* **While** the **Column-width** box is highlighted, **Type** the required width eg,**2.86, then** click the command **OK**. *The width of each selected column should adjust to the selected measurement.* Remove the highlight (see FRAME 2.8, p33).

ATTENTION We have come to the end of this lesson. **DO NOT save** this worksheet now. Please, close down Excel, then shut down Windows following the steps listed in FRAMES 1.10 and 1.11. However, if you would like to continue straight away with the next lesson, you must close down Excel now, and then restart it again.

1   With some types of data, data entry can be speeded up by making skilful use of the **Fill-handle.**

2   Unwanted data in Excel worksheet can be easily removed by using the **Cut**, **Delete** or **Clear** command from the **Edit** menu. The Delete command should always be used with caution.

3   Unwanted deletion can be easily reversed by using the **Undo** facility offered by Excel. However, it is important to remember that this facility can only be used immediately after the error has occurred.

4   Copying a document file from disk to the computer memory is called retrieving, reading or opening. When a file is copied from disk all that is effectively happening is that an image copy of that document is being read into the computer memory (ie, the RAM).

5   Before you can copy a document from disk, the disk containing the required document must be in the disk drive.

6   Besides being able to delete contents of cells, Excel allows you to insert or delete entire rows or columns. However, when deleting rows or columns of cells in this way you should always use caution. Deleting cells that contain any formulae referring to them might produce erroneous calculation.

7   You can easily increase or decrease column widths for **best fit**. Do remember that whenever you enter a number that does not fit within the display boundary of the column width, Excel stores the data but displays this number signs (###) in the cell. In this case for the full display you simply increase the column width.

8   Excel offers a number of ways to save a document to disk. It is important to use the right procedure. The <u>**Save**</u> command is used to update the old copy that has already been stored on disk. This method overwrites the old version. The **Save** <u>**As**</u> command is used to create another copy under a different name.

Warning

•   Whenever you want to use the **Save** <u>**As**</u> command to make a new version of your document you should <u>not</u> click on the **Save** icon.

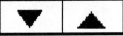
■ Start Excel for Windows.
■ Ensure your Sheet window and the Microsoft Excel window are merged into one (refer to page 20 Fig. 2.1 and 2.2) before starting any of the ensuing exercises.

*Refer to FRAMES 1.1 and 2.1 as necessary.

	At the end of this lesson you should be able to: ▼ ▲
EXERCISE4.1	1 understand how to construct formulae; 2 identify the **Standard Toolbar** and locate the sigma (Σ) icon; 3 enter formulae in cells;
EXERCISE4.2	4 identify the numeric keys on the keyboard; 5 enter numbers and test the accuracy of formulae;
EXERCISE4.3	6 identify the Standard Toolbar and locate shortcut icons for apply **bold** and *italic*; 7 select and put contents of cells in bold and italic as required;
EXERCISE4.4	8 locate on the Standard Toolbar the shortcut icons for changing the font size; 9 differentiate between the **small A** and **large A** icons; 10 increase and decrease the font size of text such as, the title in a worksheet;
EXERCISE4.5	11 identify the **Font** and **Point** boxes; 12 12change fonts and point sizes of text or numbers as required;
EXERCISE4.6	13 identify the alignment icons on the Standard Toolbar; 14 centre the contents of a cell or cells; 15 align text with the left or right border of a cell;
EXERCISE4.7	16 identify the **Number Format** dialog box; 17 change the number and currency format in your worksheet to suit your needs.
EXERCISE4.8	18 identify the Style and Shade boxes; 19 put a border round cells and shade the contents of a cell or cells; 20 hide or display the Gridlines;
EXERCISE4.9	21 use the Excel Spellchecker to proofread a worksheet;
EXERCISE4.10	22 use the Preview facilities in Excel to look at various aspects in a worksheet;
EXERCISE4.11	23 prepare the printer for printing a worksheet or other documents; 24 print single, multiple or selected pages of a worksheet.

Using formulae

A **formula** combines values with operators, such as the plus sign or the minus sign, in a cell to produce a new value from existing values.

In order to analyze data in your worksheet, you need to master the basic technique of entering a formula. With a formula you can perform a variety of calculations, such as **addition, subtraction, multiplication,** and **division,** on worksheet values. You can also perform **comparisons.**

A formula is placed in a cell like text or numbers. You must always begin a formula with an equal sign (=). It indicates to Excel that you are about to apply a formula to a cell. Figure 4.1 shows examples of formulae.

When using more than one operator with the same priority, the presence or absence of parentheses can make a difference in the result. Excel evaluates the operators from left to right. So, if you want to alter the order of evaluation, use parentheses to group expressions in your formula. Excel first calculates the expressions in parentheses, and then uses those results to calculate the formula as shown in the following examples:

Table 4.1

This formula	Produces this value
=2+4*5	22
=(2+4)*5	30

Figure 4.1 Examples of formulae

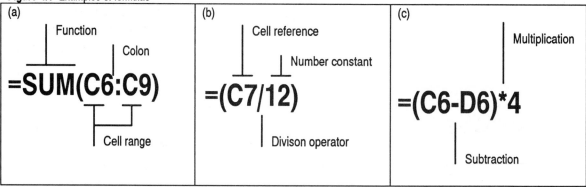

(a) Function / Colon / =SUM(C6:C9) / Cell range

(b) Cell reference / Number constant / =(C7/12) / Divison operator

(c) Multiplication / =(C6-D6)*4 / Subtraction

DO Exercise 4.1 - this will show you how to do calculations using formulae.

alternative method .....

hold down
CTRL and press
th e letter **Z**.

FRAME 4.1 Method 1

How to add a series of cells eg, cells B6 to B9

❶ Select a cell where you want the result of the addition to be recorded. (For our example select cell **B10**).

❷ Type the = sign

The = sign should appear in the Formula area.

❸ Type this formula immediately after the = sign leaving no space in between any characters:

SUM(B6:B9)

The formula should appear in the Formula area next to the = sign.

❹ Press the ENTER key.

The formula will remain in view in the Formula area but the sum should now be visible in cell B10.

FRAME 4.2 Method 2

How to add a series of cells eg, cells B6 to B9

❶ Select a cell where you want the result of the addition to be recorded. (For our example select cell **B10**).

❷ Point to the sigma icon $\boxed{\Sigma}$ and click the left mouse button.

Cells B6 to B9 should now be surrounded by a marquee. If this is indeed the case skip Step 3.

❸ Steady the Screen pointer on cell B6 and **drag** to cell B9, then release the mouse button.

Cells B6 to B9 should now be surrounded by a marquee. Before going to the next step, do check in the formula area to see that it reads =SUM(B6:B9). If not repeat Step 3.

❹ Press the ENTER key. *The sum is now visible in cell B10.*

 EXERCISE 4.1

[d] **Using the skills you have acquired do these:**

1 Add **'Expenditure for Jan. to Mar-95'** and put the result in cell **C6**. *(Clue: select cell C6 and type this formula:* =SUM(E6:G6)*)*

2 Copy the formula in cell **C6** into cells **C7**, **C8** and **C9**. *(Clue: select cell C6 - if it is not already selected - then drag the Fill-handle down to cell C9).*

3 Subtract **'Total Expend.'** from **'Annual budget'** and put the result in cell **D6** (Total Cash left). *(Clue: select cell D6 and type this formula:* =(B6-C6)*)*

4 Copy the formula in cell **D6** into cells **D7**, **D8** and **D9**. *(Clue: select cell D6 - if it is not already selected - then drag the Fill-handle down to cell D9).*

5 Copy the formula in cell **B10** into cells **C10**, **D10**, **E10**, **F10** and **G10**. *(Clue: select cell B10 and drag the Fill-handle to cell G10).*

6 Select the following cells **B13**, **B14**, **B15**, **B16** in turn and Type =SUM(C10)

7 Type a formula in cell **B17** that will **add** cells **B13 to B16**.

After the last exercise your worksheet should now look like Figure 4.2, without the highlighted cells. Cells C6 to C10 and cells E10 to G10 have a nought. This is because we have not yet entered data in cell ranges E6 to G9. If you entered the correct formula when you did the exercises in Practice box 10, cells B13 to B17 should also have a nought for now.

As we enter figures in cells E6 to G9, you will notice changes in the following cells: C6 to C9, D6 to D9, E10 to G10, and B13 to B17.

SUM is a very useful built-in Excel keyword. You should remember the following points about it.

- It eliminates the need to type the full formula eg, instead of typing: **B6+B7+B8+B9**, we are able to type: **=SUM(B6:B9)**. This is quicker if you have a lot of cells to add;
- It is expandable ie, if another row is inserted into this range of 4 cells at a later stage, the new cell would automatically be included in the range.

Furthermore:

- the expandibility feature is lost if you type the formula in full using the + sign;
- the basic procedure for amending a mistake made with a formula entry is the same as for text or numbers.

The worksheet you have created so far is ready to be used to monitor your monthly expenditure for the first three months.

DO Exercise 4.2 - it will give you an opportunity to test your worksheet.

Figure 4.2

	A	B	C	D	E	F	G
1	Northside NHS Trust hospital						
2	Princess Diana Unit						
3	Expenditure for the 1st quarter 1995						
4		Annual	Total	Total	Expend.	Expend.	Expend.
5		Budget	Expend.	Cash left	Jan-95	Feb-95	Mar-95
6	Nur.Staff	59661	0	59661			
7	Pharmacy	17771	0	17771			
8	Equip.	8219	0	8219			
9	Misc.	9020	0	9020			
10	Yr.TOTAL	94671	0	94671	0	0	0
11							
12	PROJECTION						
13	1st quart.	0					
14	2nd quart.	0					
15	3rd quart.	0					
16	4th quart.	0					
17	Yr.TOTAL	0					

[b] Select cell **E6** and type any one digit figure, then press the right arrow key.
Notice the changes in cells C6, D6, C10, D10, E10 and B13-B17.

[c] Select cell **G8** and type any one digit figure, then press the right arrow key.
Notice the changes in cells C8, D8, C10, D10, G10 and B13-B17.

[d] Select cell **E6** and press SPACEBAR then press right arrow key.
Notice the changes in cells C6, D6, C10, D10, E10 and B13-B17.

[e] Select cell **G8** and press SPACEBAR then press right arrow key.
Notice the changes in cells C8, D8, C10, D10, G10, and B13-B17.

[f] Let's add some more data to the worksheet. Follow the two simple steps below:

   1 Select cells **E6 to G9** as shown in Fig. 4.2, p62. (For a reminder on selecting multiple cells, please refer to FRAME 2.7, p33).
   Cells E6 to G9 should now be highlighted, with cell E6 ready to receive data.

   2 Start typing the figures shown below, pressing the **ENTER** key after each figure. As you press the **ENTER** key, you will be moved automatically to the next cell **downwards** until you reach cell **E9**, then you will be moved automatically to cell **F6**. When you reach cell **F9** you will again be moved automatically to cell **G6**.

   NOTE: if you make a mistake you may need to go back to step 1 and start again.

	E	F	G	
	Expend.	Expend.	Expend.	
	Jan-95	Feb-95	Mar-95	
	9662	11002	9957	
	7700	1234	837	
	4295	1200	920	
	2055	1078	800	

[g] Point to an empty cell and click the left mouse button.
The highlight on cells E6 to G9 should disappeared.

Changing the appearance of data using bold and italic tools

If you have carried out the previous exercises as instructed you should now have a functional worksheet of expenditure for the first three months. However, its overall appearance can be improved. With Excel, you can change the way your data in your worksheet looks simply by changing the alignment of text or the type and size of fonts. Some formatting commands can be found on the Format menu. However in Excel version 4.0 further formatting commands are located on the **Standard Tool bar** and **Formatting Toolbar** (Fig.4.3a); while in Excel version 5.0 they are all located on the **Formatting Toolbar** (Fig.4.3b).

Figure 4.3 shows where the **bold** and *italic* tools can be found on the Toolbar for Excel versions 4.0 and 5.0.

To put text in bold or italic, you first select the cell or range of cells containing the text, then you click the Bold or Italic icon on Toolbar.

DO Exercise 4.3 - it will show you how to format your worksheet using the bold and italic features.

Figure 4.3 Formatting Toolbars

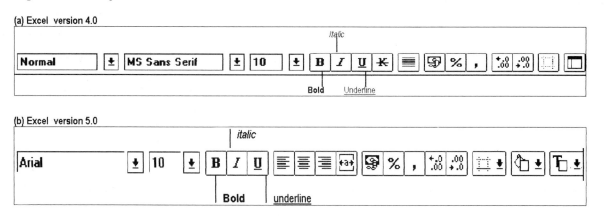

... please save the amendments you have made so

EXERCISE 4.3

[a] Ensure the Formatting toolbar is switched ON. (For help, refer to FRAME 2.3, p29).

Using the appropriate steps in FRAME 4.3:

[b] put the data in cell **A12** in bold, **then** using the same steps remove the bold.

[c] put the data in cell **B4** to **G5** in bold, **then** using the same steps remove the bold.

[d] put the title in **Row 1** in bold.

[e] [e]Put the entries in the following rows of cells in **bold**.

> Rows 2,3 (ie, the subtitles)
> Rows 4,5 (ie, headings)
> Row 10 (ie, Yr.TOTAL and all the figures)
> Row 17 (ie, Yr.TOTAL)

[f] put the entries in rows 4 and 5 in *italic*. (See Help below).

FRAME 4.3

	How to:		

Embolden entries in one cell	**Embolden entries in several cells**	**Embolden titles or subtitles**
❶ **Select** the desired cell.	❶ **Select** the desired range of cells.	❶ **Select** the **first** cell where the title or subtitle starts.
A thick border should surround the chosen cell.	*A thick border should surround the chosen cells.*	*A thick border should surround the chosen cell.*
❷ **Point** to the **bold** Icon **B** on the **Formatting Toolbar** and click the left mouse button. *Notice how the text PROJECTION is now in bold lettering.*	❷ **Point** to the **bold** Icon **B** on the **Formatting Toolbar** and click the left mouse button. *Notice that all the headings on rows 4 and 5 are now in bold.*	❷ **Point** to the **bold** Icon **B** on the **Formatting Toolbar** and click the left mouse button. *Notice that although you just selected the first cell, the whole title are in bold.*
❸ **Select** any empty cell.	❸ **Select** any empty cell.	❸ **Select** any empty cell.

N.B. To reverse the process follow the same three steps listed for the appropriate ones.

HELP

To apply italic, repeat Step 1-3 but at Step 2, click on the italic *I* icon.
To remove italic repeat Steps 1-3 but at Step 2, click on the italic icon.

Altering fonts and point sizes

Fonts and point sizes establish the basic look of characters on your worksheet. A font is a set of characters with a unique design. The following are some commonly used fonts:

Times New Roman

`Courier`

Ms Sans Serif

Each font comes in a range of sizes, measured in points. In Excel, you can specify any size from 1 point through to 409 points. For example, you can change the point size of a font, such as 'Times New Roman' from:

12 to 15

or you can change the font in a document from:

15 point Times New Roman
to
15 point Courier New
or to
12 point MS Sans Serif

To change the font size of a cell entry we will be using the facilities available on the **Formatting Toolbar** (Fig. 4.5, p68). However, if you are using Excel 4.0 you can also change font size by using the **Increase** or **Decrease Font Size** icons available on the Standard Toolbar (Fig..4.4). These icons are not normally available on any of the toolbars for Excel version 5.0. However, they can be easily added.

If you are using Excel version 5.0, before attempting Exercise 4.4, you should follow the instructions in Appendix 3 on how to create a custom toolbar and add the necessary icons to it.

 DO Exercise 4.4 - it will help you practise changing the point size of the text in your worksheet using the icons available on the Standard Toolbar or your Custom Toolbar.

Figure 4.4 The Standard Toolbar for Excel version 4.0

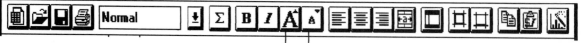

Decrease Font Size

Increase Font Size

_____ _____ 5.0 _you should do the following before_

EXERCISE 4.4 Using the worksheet _____ _____ _____ _____ _____ font size of some of the data in the worksheet.

[a] **Increase** the font size of the data in cell **A12** by following the 3-steps listed in FRAME 4.4.

[b] **Restore** the data in cell **A12** to its original size by following the information in the Help box below.

[c] **Enlarge** the font size of the subtitle in **row 3** by using the 3-steps listed in FRAME 4.5.

[d] **Return** the subtitle in row 3 to its original size.

As the font size increases, the row also increases in height to accommodate it.

FRAME 4.4

	How to make the data in a cell or range of cells bigger	

❶ **Select** the cell or range of cells
A thick border should surround the chosen cells or cells.

❷ **Point** to the large A icon, on the **Standard Toolbar or Custom Utility Toolbar**, and click the left mouse button **once**.
After a few seconds, the entry in those cell (s) should increase in size.

❸ **Select** any empty cell.

FRAME 4.5

	How to make TITLES or SUBTITLES bigger	

❶ **Select** the **Row-designator** for the desired row.
The entire row should appear on a dark background.

❷ **Point** to the large A icon, on the **Standard Toolbar or Custom Utility Toolbar**, and click the left mouse button **once**.
After a few seconds, the entry in those cell (s) should increase in size.

❸ **Select** any empty cell.

HELP

To **increase** the font size of data in cell or range of cells including titles and subtitles, you click on the **large A** icon; and to do the reverse, you click on the **small A** icon.

Large A   Small A

eg, to **decrease** the font size of data in cell(s), simply follow Steps 1-3 in FRAME 4.4 or 4.5 as appropriate, BUT at Step 2 click once on the **small A** icon.

Altering fonts and point sizes (contd)

The fonts and point sizes which are available depend on the printer you are using and are shown in the **Font** and **Points** boxes on the **Formatting Toolbar** (Fig.4.5). When you:

click on the down arrow ⊞ for the Font and Point,

an extended list is displayed.

You will find :

point **10** or **12** the most useful for all cell entries.

point **16** or **20** useful for titles

You change font and point size by first selecting the cell or cells and then clicking on the appropriate font or point size. If the size you want is not listed, type the size in the **Points box**.

DO Exercise 4.5 - it will help you practise changing the font type and point size in your worksheet using the icons available on the Formatting Toolbar.

Figure 4.5 Formatting Toolbars

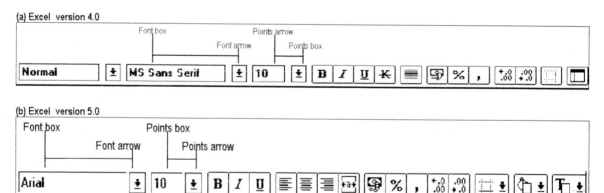

following the 3-steps in FRAME 4.6

[c] As we did not really want to change the font in this worksheet, use the command **Undo** to reverse the process.

[d] **Change** the point size of the data in cell **A17** by following the 3-steps in FRAME 4.7

[e] Use the command **Undo** and restore the original point size for the data in cell **A17**.

[f] **Using the skills you have acquired above, do the following:**

1 **Reduce** the font size of the contents in cells **B4 to G4** to 8 points.
2 **Increase** the font size of the contents in **row 1** to 18 points.
3 **Increase** the font size of the contents in **row 2** to 16 points.
4 **Increase** the font size of the contents in **row 3** to 14 points.
5 **Select** cells **A6 to A9**, and **decrease** the font size of the contents of those cells to 8 points, then remove the highlight.

2. To **Undo** a change, **Hold down** the CTRL key and press **Z**.

FRAME 4.6

	Changing the font	

❶ **Select** the desire cell or cells.
A thick border should surround the chosen cell(s).

❷ Steady the screen pointer on the down arrow

Times New Roman ⬇ of the **Font box** icon and click the left mouse button.
An extended list of fonts should appear.

❸ **Point** to one of the several fonts listed in the extended menu list and click the left mouse button.
The contents of the chosen cell should now look different.

FRAME 4.7

▬	Changing the point size	▼ ▲

❶ **Select** the desired cell or cells.
A thick border should surround the chosen cell(s).

❷ Steady the screen pointer on the 12 ⬇ down arrow of the **Points box** icon, then click on the left mouse button.
An extended list of font sizes should appear.

❸ **Point** to one of the several font sizes listed in the extended menu list and click the left mouse button.
The contents of the chosen cell should have altered in size.

HELP

Here is an alternative way to change point size:

1 steady screen pointer on Points box;
2 double-click the left mouse button;
3 type the required number eg, **18**;
4 press the ENTER key.

 **INFO**

Aligning data in a worksheet

In Excel, text is automatically aligned to the left in a cell and numbers are aligned to the right. However, using the alignment tools available on the **Toolbar**, you can align the data the way you want. For example, you can choose to align entries in the left, right or centre of a cell or even centre text across columns.

Being able to use the alignment features can help to make your worksheet look neater. For example, you will be able to quickly centre cell headings, worksheet titles and subtitles, or flush non-numeric data to the right of a cell as desired.

There are several methods that can be used to align data. In this workbook we are going to use the tools on theToolbar (Fig. 4.6).

The process is simple. You select the cell or cells you want to format and click the appropriate alignment icon. On Excel version 4.0 the align icons or tools can be located on the **Standard Toolbar**, while for Excel version 5.0, they can be found on the **Formatting Toolbar**. (See Figures 4.6a and 4.6b).

DO Exercise 4.6 - this will teach you how to use alignment features with your worksheet.

Figure 4.6 Location of Alignment tools for Excel versions 4.0 and 5.0

(a) Excel version 4.0 - Standard Toolbar

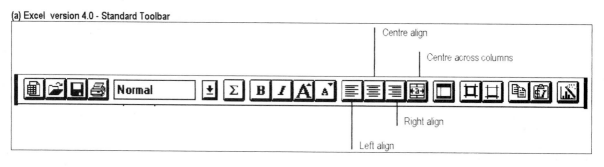

(b) Excel version 5.0 - Formatting Toolbar

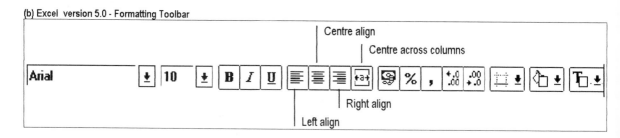

[b] Following the 3-steps in FRAME 4.9 below, centre the ~~~~~ between column **A and G**. (*Clue: you need to select cell A2 to G2*).

[c] Return the subtitle in **row 2** to its original position (*Clue: follow the same 3-steps you took in [b] above*).

[d] **Applying the skills you have learnt above do the following:**

1 **Centre** the title in **row 1** between columns **A and G**.
2 **Centre** the subtitle in **row 2** between columns **A and G**.
3 **Select** cells **A6 to A9** and align the text to the right side of column **A**.
4 **Select** cells **A13 to A16** and align the text to the right side of column **A**.

FRAME 4.8

How to:		
align text with the right border of a column	**Centre text**	**align text with the left border of a column**
❶ Select the cell or cells *The cell(s) is highlighted and surrounded with a thick border.* ❷ Click on the **Right Aligned Text** icon located on the **Toolbar**. ⊟ *The text in the cells is aligned with the right border.* ❸ Select any empty cell.	❶ Select the cell or cells *The cell(s) is highlighted and surrounded with a thick border.* ❷ Click on the **Centred Text** icon located on the **Toolbar**. ⊟ *Each line of the text is centred within the column* ❸ Select any empty cell.	❶ Select the cell or cells *The cell(s) is highlighted and surrounded with a thick border.* ❷ Click on the **Left-Aligned Text** icon located on the **Toolbar**. ⊟ *The text is aligned with the left border of the column* ❸ Select any empty cell.

FRAME 4.9

How to centre text across selected columns
❶ Select the range of cells required. *The selected cells should appear on a dark background surrounded by a thick border.* ❷ Point to this **Centred** ⊞ icon located on the Toolbar and click the left mouse button. *The selected text should centre itself between the columns A and G.* ❸ Select any empty cell to remove the highlight.

NOTE: To reverse the process, you simply repeat Steps 1-3.

Formatting data in your worksheet using the Number Format option

When you create a new worksheet, Excel automatically uses the General number format unless you instruct it to do otherwise. Excel includes a variety of number, date and time formats which you can choose from. For example, you can choose the code 0.00 from the list in the **Number Format** dialog box (Fig. 4.7), if you want the currency numbers in your worksheet to be displayed to 2 decimal places. If you are not satisfied with the built-in formats, Excel allows you to create your own custom format.

To alter the way numeric values are displayed, you first select all the numeric cells, then select the **Number** command. When the Number Format dialog box appears you can then select the appropriate category or codes (Fig. 4.7).

The Number Format dialog box for Excel version 4.0 is slightly different to that of version 5.0. (See Figure 4.7)

DO Exercise 4.7 - this will show you how to change the currency format in your current worksheet.

Figure 4.7a   Number Format dialog box for Excel version 4.0

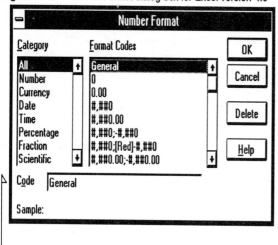

This is where you can type your customized symbol

Number Format dialog box for Excel version 5.0

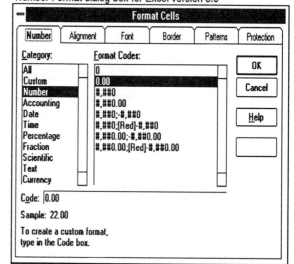

...the worksheet **MYTASK3**, practise using the **Number Format** by

---

How to use the Number Format   ▼ ▲

❶ **Select** the cell or range of cells required.
The cell or range of cells required should now be highlighted.

❷ **Steady** the Screen pointer on one of the **selected cells** and click the **RIGHT** mouse button. *A command list should appear.*

❸ For Excel version 4.0, **point** to the command **Number** and click the left mouse button. *A Number Format dialog box should appear.*

For Excel version 5.0, **point** to the command **Format Cells** and click the left mouse button. *A Format Cells dialog box should appear.*

❹ **Point** to the **0.00** option and click the left mouse button to highlight it.

❺ **Point** to the command **OK** and click the left mouse button.

All the figures should now display upto 2 decimal places as you would expect with pounds and pence. However, if a series of hashes #### appear in some of the cells, this is because the column width is too narrow. The width will need to be adjusted.

❻ Remove the highlight.

> When ever a number does not fit within the display boundary of the column width, Excel displays the number signs: #####

EXERCISE 4.7

[b] **Enlarge** the width of columns **B to G** so that all the figures in a these columns can be displayed in full. *(Clue: Select columns B to G, then follow Steps 2 to 4 of **Method 1** in FRAME 3.18, p57).*

[c] **For further practice do the following:**
Change the width of **column A** to fit the contents of cell **A10**. *(Clue: follow Steps 1-3 of **Method 2** in FRAME 3.18, p57).*

[d] **Save** this worksheet under its current name to your floppy disk, using the steps listed in FRAME 3.16 or 3.17, p55.

[e] **Rename** this worksheet and called it **MYTASK3B**. (For help see FRAME 3.11, p49).

HELP

You should always use the **Number Format** option to add currency symbols. Do not enter currency symbols directly. If you do, Excel will regard the values as text, not numbers, and it will not be able to use them in calculations. If your version of Excel is not set up to show the pound sign, you can type it in directly into the **Code box** (Fig.4.7), when the **Number Format** dialog box appears.

 # Borders, Shading and Gridlines

Excel allows you to shade cells or put a border around them. You can use borders and shades to mark off various sections of the worksheet and make it easier to read. Borders and shades can be further emphasized by turning off the gridlines marking the cell boundaries. Compare Figures 4.8 and 4.9 below.

DO Exercise 4.8 - it will assist you putting borders and shades, and show you how to turn off the gridlines.

Figure 4.8

Northside NHS Trust hospital
Princess Diana Unit
Expenditure for the 1st quarter 1995

	Annual Budget	Total Expend.	Total Cash left	Expend. Jan-95	Expend. Feb-95	Expend. Mar-95
Nur.Staff	59661.00	30621.00	29040.00	9662.00	11002.00	9957.00
Pharmacy	17771.00	9771.00	8000.00	7700.00	1234.00	837.00
Equip.	8219.00	6415.00	1804.00	4295.00	1200.00	920.00
Misc.	9020.00	3933.00	5087.00	2055.00	1078.00	800.00
Yr.TOTAL	94671.00	50740.00	43931.00	23712.00	14514.00	12514.00
PROJECTION						
1st quart.	50740					
2nd quart.	50740					
3rd quart.	50740					
4th quart.	50740					
Yr.TOTAL	202960					

Figure 4.9

Northside NHS Trust hospital
Princess Diana Unit
Expenditure for the 1st quarter 1995

	Annual Budget	Total Expend.	Total Cash left	Expend. Jan-95	Expend. Feb-95	Expend. Mar-95
Nur.Staff	59661.00	30621.00	29040.00	9662.00	11002.00	9957.00
Pharmacy	17771.00	9771.00	8000.00	7700.00	1234.00	837.00
Equip.	8219.00	6415.00	1804.00	4295.00	1200.00	920.00
Misc.	9020.00	3933.00	5087.00	2055.00	1078.00	800.00
Yr.TOTAL	94671.00	50740.00	43931.00	23712.00	14514.00	12514.00

PROJECTION	
1st quart.	50740
2nd quart.	50740
3rd quart.	50740
4th quart.	50740
Yr.TOTAL	202960

...TASK3P follow the

Remember

[a] Hide the gridlin...

FRAME 4.11

How to:		
put a border around an area	**shade an area**	**hide gridlines**

put a border around an area	shade an area	hide gridlines
❶ **Select** the required cell or range of cells. *When properly selected, the range of cells will appear on a dark background.* Steady the Screen pointer on any one of the darkened cell and click the **RIGHT** button. *An extended command list should appear.* **For Excel version 4.0** Point to the command **Border** and click the left mouse button. *A Border dialog box should appear.* **For Excel version 5.0** (a) Point to the command **Format Cells** and click the left mouse button. *A Format Cells dialog box should appear.* (b) Point to the command **Border** and click the left mouse button. **Notice** the **8 boxes** under **Style**. *These are the different styles you can choose to frame the contents of cells.* Point to one of the **Style boxes** with solid line and click the left mouse button. *A thick rectangle should surround that box.* ❻ Point to the **white rectangular box** next to the command **Outline** and click the left mouse button. *The chosen style should appear in the white box.* ❼ Point to the command **OK** and click the left mouse button, then remove the highlight. *A border should now surround the chosen area.*	❶ **Select** the required cell or range of cells. *When properly selected, the range of cells will appear on a dark background.* Steady the Screen pointer on any one of the darkened cell and click the **RIGHT** button. *An extended command list should appear.* **For Excel version 4.0** (a) Point to the command **Border** and click the left mouse button. *A Border dialog box should appear.* (b) Point to the square box labelled Shade and click the left mouse button. *An x should appear in the box.* **For Excel version 5.0** (a) Point to the command **Format Cells** and click the left mouse button. *A Format Cells dialog box should appear.* (b) Point to the command **Patterns** and click the left mouse button. (c) Point to a particular shade/colour and click the left mouse button. Point to the command **OK** and click the left mouse button, then remove the highlight. *This row of cells should now be shaded·.*	❶ **For Excel version 4.0** (a) Steady the Screen pointer on the command **Options** located on the Menu bar and click the left mouse button. *An extended command list should appear.* (b) Steady the Screen pointer on the command **Display** and click the left mouse button or **D.** *A "Display Options" dialog box should appear.* **For Excel version 5.0** (a) Steady the Screen pointer on the command **Tools** located on the Menu bar and click the left mouse button. *An extended command list should appear.* (b) Steady the Screen pointer on the command **Options** and click the left mouse button. *A dialog box should appear.* Steady the Screen pointer on the box labelled **Gridlines** and click the left mouse button. *The x in the box should disappear.* Point to the command **OK** and click the left mouse button. *All gridlines in the worksheet should have disappeared displaying only the borders.*

Using the Spellchecker

In previous lessons you learned how to use various keys to make corrections. You can also get Excel to check the spelling of a word or of your entire worksheet for spelling errors. Unless a range is selected when you choose the **Spelling** command, Excel checks the entire worksheet. Excel Spellchecker compares your worksheet against words in its standard dictionary. If a word is not found in this dictionary, the word is displayed in the **Spelling** dialog box (Fig. 4.10) so that you can correct the possible misspelling.

OVERVIEW OF SPELLCHECKER

When Excel displays a word it does not recognize, you have a number of options. You can choose:

Ignore to leave the word unchanged.

Ignore All to leave all occurrences of the word unchanged.

Change to change the word to the word in the **Change To** box.

Change All to change all occurrences of the word to the word in the **Change To** box.

Add to include the word to the dictionary in the **Add Words To** box.

Excel also allows you to choose:

Suggest to display a list of suggestions after you have typed a word in the **Change To** box.

Cancel to close the dialog box. (Note: the **Cancel** box changes to **Close** when you perform an action that Excel cannot reverse.)

DO Exercise 4.9 - it should help you correct any possible misspellings in the worksheet **MYTASK3B**.

Figure 4.10 The Spellchecker dialog box for Excel version 5.0

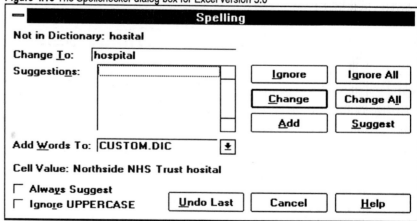

... ...listed in FRAME 4.12 and check your worksheet for incorrect

❶ Select cell **A1**. *A thick rectangular border should appear around the cell.*

❷ **For Excel version 4.0:** Steady the Screen pointer on the Command **Options** situated on the Menu bar and click the left mouse button. *An extended command list should appear.*

For Excel version 5.0: Steady the Screen pointer on the Command **Tools** situated on the Menu bar and click the left mouse button. *An extended command list should appear.*

❸ Steady the Screen pointer on the Command **Spelling** and click the left mouse button.

A Spelling dialog box should appear and Excel would have started checking the worksheet for misspellings. It will display the first word it does not recognize in the Spelling dialog box and (sometimes) suggests an alternative in the Change To box, which you can accept or ignore.

❹ **At this point do one of the following:**

▷ if you agree with the suggested correction in the **Change To** box, steady the Screen pointer on the **Change** or **Change All** button and click the left mouse button. *Excel will correct the word or all instances of the same word.*

▷ if you are satisfied with the current spelling, click on the **Ignore** or **Ignore all** button. *Excel will leave the word unaltered and move to the next unrecognized word if any.*

▷ to specify a different correction, select a word from the **Suggestions** list by double-clicking on it or by typing the new word in the **Change To** box then clicking on **Change** or **Change All**. *Excel will correct the word or all instances of the same word.*

❺ When Excel has finished checking the entire worksheet another dialog box should appear. Click on the command **OK.**

1. Excel does not check protected worksheets.

2. If the selected cell was not at the beginning of your worksheet when you began the spell check, Excel asks if you want to continue checking from the beginning of the worksheet. Click the YES or NO button as appropriate.

3. You can also check the spelling in a worksheet or a selected word using the Spelling tool on the Utility toolbar.

HELP

The dictionary, although large, may not always contain an identified word. When Excel encounters a word that is not part of the standard dictionary, it flags it up. If the word is correct, you can ask Excel to add it to the dictionary by clicking on the **Add** button. Excel will then remember this word in the future.

Previewing a worksheet

Excel allows you see your worksheet on the screen before you print it on paper (see Fig. 4.11). This have several advantages:

- you can see each page exactly as it will be printed;
- you can check if it has the correct margins, page breaks and page number;
- you can check if the headers and footers are in the right place.

If you do not like what you see you can make the necessary adjustments before printing your worksheet, thus saving you time and stops you wasting paper. You can preview your worksheet in **Full-page view** or **Actual-size view**. The Full-page view will appear first, showing you an entire page on the screen. If you want a closer look at the page, you can enlarge the page to actual size by using the **Zoom button** (Fig. 4.11). This works like a toggle switch, allowing you to switch between these two views of your worksheet. You cannot edit the contents of the worksheet here, though it is possible to adjust the margins by dragging the **Margin handles** (Fig. 4.11). Using the **Scroll bar** you can also move between pages. Take a look at Figure 4.11. It shows the worksheet, **MYTASK3**. Notice the buttons that have been labelled then do the exercise suggested below.

Figure 4.11 The Excel Print Preview window

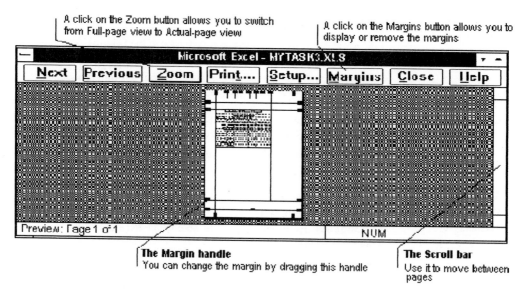

DO **Exercise 4.10**   it will help you preview the worksheet you created in the last lesson. **Do not** use any functions you are not asked to for now.

Using the worksheet **MYTASK3B** do the following:

FRAME 4.13

How to shift from Normal view to Preview mode

❶ Steady the Screen pointer on the command **File** on the **Menu bar** and click on the left mouse button. *An extended command list should appear.*

❷ **Point** to the **Print Preview** and click the left mouse button, or press the letter **V**. *A Sandtimer should appear. After a moment the screen will change to display the worksheet as it will appear when printed.*

❸ **Notice** the 8 buttons labelled, **Next, Previous, Zoom, Print, Setup, Margins, Close, Help.**

Remember

The **Next** button is unavailable when the last page is displayed, and the **Previous** button is unavailable when the first page is displayed.

How to display and adjust top margin	How to switch from full page to actual size view
❹ **Point** to the button labelled **Margins** and click the left mouse button (or press the letter **M**). *The margins should be visible.*	❹ **Point** to the button labelled **Zoom** and click the left mouse button (or press the letter **Z**). *The worksheet should enlarge giving you an actual-size view.*
❺ **Position** the Screen pointer on the **horizontal Margin handle** (see Fig.4.11). *It should changed to a Double-headed arrow.*	❺ **Repeat** Step **4**. *The worksheet should revert back to full-page view.*
❻ **Drag** the top horizontal **Margin-handle** downwards. *The Sandtimer should appear. After a few seconds the contents of the worksheet should shift downwards.*	❻ **Position** the Screen pointer on an area of the worksheet, **eg**, on a cell. *The shape of the Screen pointer should change to a magnifying glass.*
❼ **Repeat** Step **6**, but this time drag the top horizontal Margin handle **upwards.**	❼ Now, while holding the Screen pointer steady **click** on the left mouse button. *The chosen area is magnifies giving you a closer view.*
❽ **Repeat** Step **4**, to hide the margins.	❽ Repeat Step 4 to revert to full-page view.

 EXERCISE 4.10 [d] Save a copy of **MYTASK3B** to your floppy disk, using the steps listed in FRAME 3.16 or 3.17, p55. This way if for one reason or another you should lose the document during printing, you can load a duplicate copy from your disk. This is a habit well worth cultivating.

Printing a worksheet

If your printer is in good working order, is properly connected with the appropriate setup options, is **on-line**, and has paper in it, then printing is very easy. You simply:

point and click on the **Printer** icon 🖨 located on the **Standard Toolbar**.

This method is fine as long as you want to print all of the pages in your worksheet. However, if you have a worksheet consisting of several pages and you only want to print a few of them, or you want to print more than one copy, you will need to use a more elaborate approach which requires you to type the specific information, in the **Print** dialog box (See Fig. 4.12), so that Excel can control the printing.

Familiarize yourself with Figure 4.12. Notice the parts that have been labelled, then do the exercise suggested.

Figure 4.12 The Print dialog box

You click on this button when you
are ready to print

If you need
more than one
copy you
double-click
in this box and
type the number
of copies you
want or
click on the
arrows next
to the box.

Print

Printer: BJ200 on LPT1:
Print What
   ○ **Selection**
   ◉ **Selected Sheet(s)**
   ○ **Entire Workbook**

Copies: 1

Page Range
   ◉ **All**
   ○ **Page(s) From:** [ ] **To:** [ ]

| OK |
| Cancel |
| Page Setup... |
| Print Preview |
| Printer Setup... |
| Help |

Enter starting page in this box   Enter end page in this box

💻 **DO Exercise 4.11**   it will take you through the process of printing your worksheet.

... FRAME 4.14 or those in FRAME 4.15, print your

Excel now, and then restart it ...

FRAME 4.14

 How to print all the pages

❶ Ensure your printer is (a) properly connected to your computer, (b) loaded with paper, (c) plugged in, (d) switched on, and (e) the green light next to the **on-line** button is lit up.
When the on-line light is on, it indicates that the printer is ready to receive your worksheet for printing.

❷ Steady the Screen pointer on the **Printer** icon on the **Standard Toolbar** and click the left mouse button. *A dialog box should appear indicating that the computer is passing on your worksheet to the printer for printing.*

FRAME 4.15

How to print selected pages

❶ Ensure your printer is (a) properly connected to your computer, (b) loaded with paper, (c) plugged in, (d) switched on, and (e) the green light next to the **on-line** button is lit up.

❷ Press the **ALT** key once, then press the letter **F**, or steady the Screen pointer on the word **File** on the **Menu bar** and click the left mouse button. *An extended command list should appear.*

❸ Press on the letter **P**, or steady the Screen pointer on the command **Print** and click the left mouse button. *A Print dialog box (Fig.4.12) should appear.*

❹ Steady the Screen pointer on the **circle** labelled **Pages** and click the left mouse button. *A black dot should appear inside the white circle and the cursor should have jumped to the box labelled From.*

❺ Type the **page number** where you want printing to start from. For our purpose type **1**, then press **TAB** key once.
The cursor should jump to the box labelled To.

❻ Type the **page number** where you want printing to stop. For our purpose type **1**, then press **TAB** key once.

❼ Steady the point in the box labelled **Copies** and **double-click** the left mouse button, then type the **number of copies** you want. For our purpose type **1**, then press **TAB** key onc. *A dotted frame should appear around the button labelled OK*

❽ Press **ENTER**, or click on the **OK** button.
A Printing dialog box should appear indicating that the computer is passing your worksheet to the printer.

Remember

1. Always **Preview** you worksheet before printing, this way you will know what you are getting.

2. If Excel is having problems printing your document you may get a message informing you what the problem is and what action you should take. If not, check that the printer is on-line, the paper tray is not empty, the ribbon or cartridge is not missing or used up, the printer cable is not disconnected. If you are using a network in the college, enlist the help of the IT lecturer or Technician.

1 Excel allows you to carry a variety of calculations using formulae. The technique of entering a formula in the worksheet is quite simple and easy to learn. Formulae can equally be deleted with ease using the **Delete** command, though caution is required.

2 There is a shortcut **SUM** function available on the **Standard Toolbar** represented by the Sigma (Σ) icon. This function eliminates the need to type the full formula into a cell. This function is also expandable ie, if another row is inserted into that range of cells at a later stage, the new cell would automatically be included in the range.

3 In Excel you can improve the presentation of your data on the worksheet by making use of a variety of features including, **bold**, *italic*, **borders, shades, alternative fonts** and **point sizes**.

4 When entering data in the worksheet, text are automatically aligned to the left, while numbers are aligned to the right in cells. However, using the alignment features available on the **Standard Toolbar**, you can change this to suit your own needs. Text or numbers can be aligned to the left, right or even placed in the centre of cells.

5 Although when starting a new worksheet, Excel assigns a general number format to numeric values, the way they are eventually displayed is very much under your control. You decide the format and then you instruct Excel accordingly, via the **Number Format** dialog box.

6 You can quickly and efficiently proof read you worksheet using the Spellchecker. However, the Excel dictionary, although large, may not always contain an identified word. By using the **Add** facility though, Excel can be taught to remember new words, thus increasing the vocabulary of the dictionary.

7 Worksheets charts and so on can be viewed on the screen and adjustments made before printing.

8 Printing a worksheet or chart is as simple as clicking on the **Printer** icon, situated on the Standard Toolbar. It is also possible to print selected pages or to instruct Excel to print multiple copies of the same worksheets or charts or any other documents you have created.

- You should never enter currency symbols such as, £s and pence directly into cells. If you do, Excel will regard the values as text instead of numbers. Always use the Number Format dialog box.
- Never attempt to print a worksheet before you have saved a copy on disk. Printers can sometimes lock up the machine, hence there is always a chance you will lose your work.

memory until you are instructed to do so. Simply
- switch on the computer and monitor now and load Windows 3.1*
- start Excel for Windows*
- Ensure your Sheet window and the Microsoft Excel window are merged into one (refer to page 26 Fig. 2.1 and 2.2) before starting any of the ensuing exercises.

*Refer to FRAMES 1.1 and 2.1 as necessary.

	At the end of this lesson you should be able to: ▼ ▲
EXERCISE5.1	1 Understand the difference between **Embedded chart** and **Chart document**; 2 Create an Embedded chart;
EXERCISE5.2	3 Recognize an Embedded chart; 4 Update and relocate an Embedded chart; 5 Change an Embedded chart for a different type;
EXERCISE5.3	6 Differentiate between the **worksheet window** mode and the **chart window** mode; 7 Shift from worksheet window mode to chart window mode as required; 8 Change the size of an embedded chart;
EXERCISE5.4	9 Recognize the Text dialog box; 10 Add text to a chart;
EXERCISE5.5	11 Saving an Embedded chart with the source worksheet; 12 Saving an Embedded chart on its own as a Chart document; 13 Close down a file without closing down Excel;
EXERCISE5.6	14 List two advantages of a Chart document as compared to an Embedded chart; 15 Create a **Chart document**; 16 Add a Legend to a chart;
EXERCISE5.7	17 Open and existing chart; 18 Shift from worksheet window mode to chart window mode and vice versa as required;

Using charts to represent data

The data in your worksheet can be graphically represented using charts. Excel version 4.0 lets you create14 types of charts - 8 two-dimensional (2-D) chart types and 6 three-dimensional (3-D) chart types; while Excel version 5.0 lets you create15 types of charts (see Fig. 5.4, p86). In addition you can create your own types. Once you have selected the data you want to plot, you can create the chart **directly on the worksheet** (called embedded chart), or **as a separate document in its own window** (called chart document).

- **Embedded chart.** This can be easily created using the **ChartWizard** tool on the Standard toolbar or the **Chart** toolbar (Fig. 5.3, p86).
- **Chart document** in a separate window can be created using the command **New** on the **File** menu.

You should create embedded chart if you want it to be displayed or printed with worksheet data. However, all charts - embedded or not - are linked to the source worksheet and are always updated when you update the source data.

DO Exercise 5.1 - it will show you step-by-step how to create an **Embedded Column-chart** for the 1st quarter's expenditures using the worksheet you created in the previous lesson.

Figure 5.1
Standard toolbar showing the location of the ChartWizard tool for Excel versions 4.0 and 5.0

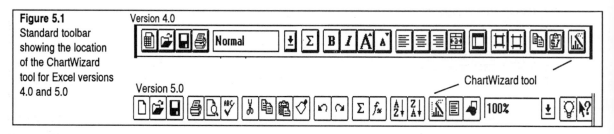

Figure 5.2

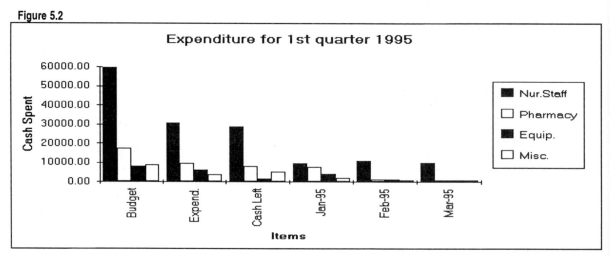

We are going to create a standard column chart. Excel will

Remember

FRAME 3.10, p49)

[b] Rename the worksheet as **MYTASK4**. (For help, see FRAME 3.11, p49).

[c] Follow the **6-steps** listed in FRAME 5.1 below, and create an **embedded column-chart** using the data in cell range **A5** to **G9**.

FRAME 5.1

| How to create an embedded column-chart on a worksheet with the ChartWizard tool | |

❶ Select the appropriate range of cells containing the data you want to use to creat your chart, (eg, **A5** to **G9**).
The selected cells should appear on a dark background.

Steady the Screen pointer on the **ChartWizard** [icon] tool located on the **Standard toolbar** and click the left mouse button. *The selected cells will be surrounded by a marquee and the pointer should take the shape of a cross hair.*

To mark the area where the chart will eventually appear, **steady** the Screen pointer in the centre of cell **F16** and **drag** **upwards** and **leftwards** until you reach the top of the left corner of cell **A1**, then release the mouse button.
After a few seconds, a ChartWizard dialog box should appear.

Look at the box labelled **Range**, and verify that you have selected the correct range of cells.
Assuming you are using the cell range given as example in Step 1 above, it should read $A$5:$G$9 (on Excel version 4.0) and = $A$5:$G$9 (on Excel version 5.0). If this is correct go to Step 5, otherwise click on Cancel and start again at Step 1.

The **ChartWizard** dialog box will appear five times. Each time it will display a different sample chart. Each time it appears, steady the Screen pointer on the command **NEXT** and click the left mouse button until it reaches **Step 5 of 5.**

❻ When the **ChartWizard** dialog box shows **Step 5 of 5**, press the letter **C** on the keyboard **once**.
The cursor should now be flashing ing in the Chart title box.

❼ **Now** do the following:

ꞌ   In the **Chart title** box, type **Expenditure for 1st quarter 1995**, then press the TAB key.

ꞌ   In the **Category(X)** box, type **items**, then press the TAB key.

ꞌ   In the **Value Y** box, type **Cash Spent**, and press ENTER or click the command **Finish** or **OK.**

N.B *After a few seconds, you should see a chart superimposed on your worksheet. The **Chart toolbar** (Fig. 5.3, p86) will automatically switch on at this point.*

| ? HELP | Each column in the chart (Fig. 5.2) represents one of the cell values that you selected on the worksheet. The chart shows the **Annual budget, Total Expenditure for the first quarter, Total cash left, Expenditure of Jan-95, Feb-95** and **Mar-95**, for each of the following items: **Nursing Staff, Pharmacy, Equipment** and **Miscellaneous** spending. |

As mentioned already, Excel allows you to create a variety of charts. Once an embedded chart is created, it can be **updated**, **relocated**, **resized**, or even **changed** for a different type.

On Excel version 4.0 the Chart toolbar is a long strip displaying all the different types of chart available. This toolbar will appear automatically after using the ChartWizard tool. However, in Excel version 5.0 the Chart toolbar is a shorter strip. Clicking on the down arrow exposes a list of the available charts. (See Fig. 5.3 below).

After an embedded chart is created, if you are not satisfied with it or do not require it any more, you can also get rid of it by using the commands **Cut** or **Clear**.

DO Exercise 5.2 - this will show you step-by-step how to update. relocate and change an embedded chart.

Figure 5.3a

Chart Toolbar for Excel versions, showing the location of the tools for various types of charts.

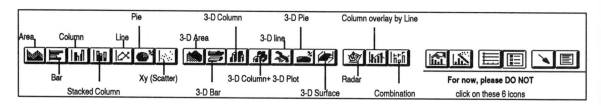

Figure 5.3b

Chart Toolbar for Excel version 5.0. To reveal the chart type icons you should click on the arrow as indicated.

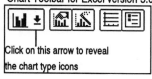

Figure 5.4

Here are the 15 types of charts that Excel version 5.0 allows you to create. On Excel version 4.0, the Doughnut type is not available.

Area	Bar	Column	Line	Pie
Radar	XY (Scatter)	Combination	3-D Area	3-D Bar
3-D Column	3-D Line	3-D Pie	3-D Surface	Doughnut

Using the worksheet **MYTASK4**, do the following:

[c] Before moving on, please ensure the content of cell ...

[d] Use the steps listed in FRAME 5.3 and practise relocating your chart.

FRAME 5.2

	How to update an embedded chart	

❶ Select the desired cell. *When the cell is correctly selected its contents will appear in the Formula area*.

❷ Type the **new** figure, then press the ENTER key. *The chart changes in response to the new data entry*.

NOTE:

To view the changes again, use the **Undo** facility.

(**Clue**: hold down CTRL then press the letter **Z**.) *Each time you undo, you will see the change in your chart*.

FRAME 5.3

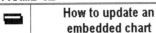	How to relocate an embedded chart	

❶ Steady the Screen pointer in the **centre** of the chart.

❷ **Drag** the chart to the **right**, then release the mouse button. *The chart moves to a new position towards the right of the worksheet*.

❸ Repeat Step 2, but this time **drag downwards**. *The chart moves to a new position towards the end of the work sheet*.

❹ Repeat Step 2, but now **drag** to the **left**. *The chart moves to a new position towards the left of the worksheet*.

❺ Position the chart on the worksheet in a place of your choice.

 **EXERCISE 5.2**

[e] Take a look at the **Chart toolbar** on your screen (you may need to switch it on. For help, refer to FRAME 2.3, p29).

[f] Now, follow the steps listed in FRAME 5.4 below and practise changing the chart for different ones. (**NOTE**: for the moment, please click **only** on those that I have labelled).

[g] Change your chart back to a column chart before moving on (see Fig. 5.2).

FRAME 5.4

	How to change an embedded chart type	

Remember

To **delete** a chart, position the Screen pointer on it and click the **RIGHT** mouse button, then click on the command **Clear**

❶ Steady the Screen pointer in the chart and click the left mouse button. *Eight small squares should appear on the vertical and horizontal lines framing the chart*.

❷ **For Excel version 4.0**, identify the chart toolbar. *You should usually find it at the top or bottom of your screen*.

For Excel version 5.0, click on the arrow on the toolbar labelled in Fig. 5.3b, to reveal the chart type icons.

❸ Steady the Screen pointer on the desired tool icon on the Chart toolbar and click the left mouse button. *The chart is re-plotted*.

❹ To change the chart for another type, repeat Step 3.

Excel version 4.0 - If you are using this version of Excel, you can shift between the **worksheet window containing the embedded chart** to the **chart window mode** which will contain only the chart. You will know you are in the chart window mode when the label **Chart** is written after the filename of the worksheet on the title bar. Take a look at Figure 5.4 below - it shows you what a chart window looks like. Compare this figure with your current window on your screen and spot the difference.

Regardless which version of Excel you are using, it allows you to resize your embedded chart as desired. The next exercise gives you the opportunity to do this.

DO Exercise 5.3 - it will show you step-by-step how to resize an embedded chart and (**for Users of version 4.0 only**) how to move from the worksheet window to the chart window mode and vice versa.

Figure 5.4 Chart window mode in Excel version 4.0

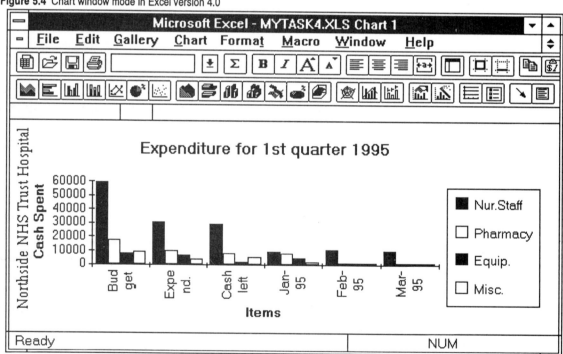

How to resize an embedded chart

❶ Steady the Screen pointer in the centre of the chart and click the left mouse button. *You should now see eight small squares positioned on the vertical and horizontal lines framing the chart. The presence of these squares indicate that the chart is selected.*

❷ Steady the Screen pointer on one of the small squares located in one of the **corners** of the frame. *When positioned correctly, the pointer changes to a **Double-headed** arrow.*

❸ **Drag** inwards. *The chart should reduce in size.*

❹ **Drag** outwards. *The chart increases in size.*

Remember

To select an embedded chart, steady the Screen pointer on and click the left mouse button.

EXERCISE 5.3

To be carried out by Users of Excel version 4.0 only.

[c] Using the steps listed in FRAME 5.6, practise shifting between **worksheet window mode** and **chart window mode** until you feel comfortable with the procedure.

[d] Ensure you are in the **chart window mode** before moving on.

FRAME 5.6 - These Steps will only work with Excel version 4.0

How to shift from:	
worksheet to chart window	**chart to worksheet window**
❶ Steady the Screen pointer in the centre of the embedded-chart and **Double-click** the left mouse button. *After a moment, the screen will change to the **chart window.** The embedded chart will have covered the worksheet completely. The filename on the title bar will have the label **Chart** written after it.*	❶ Steady the Screen pointer on the command **Window**, situated on the **Menu bar,** and click the left mouse button. *An extended command list should appear showing the name of your **worksheet** and the name of the **worksheet chart**.* ❷ Steady the Screen pointer on the name of your worksheet and click the left mouse button. *Your chosen worksheet should appear again.*

Adding text on a chart

In Excel you are able to correct or add further text directly on the chart. For example, you can correct a title or a label or add a comment. The procedure for correcting or adding text is simple. Read this overview below before doing the exercise on the facing page.

OVERVIEW OF THE STEPS FOR ADDING TEXT

For Excel version 4.0, **First** get in the chart window mode. *The cursor should already be waiting in the Formula Area.*

For Excel version 5.0, **First** Double-click on the chart. *If done correctly, the chart will be surrounded by a thick-striped frame.*

Type your text in the Formula area.

Press the ENTER key. *The text should appear on the chart enclosed by handles (ie, small black squares.*

Use the handles to make the text bigger or smaller.

Format the text using the desired font and point size.

Select and drag the text to move it to a location of your choice.

OVERVIEW OF THE STEPS FOR CORRECTING TEXT

For Excel version 4.0, **First** get in the chart window mode. *The cursor should already be waiting in the Formula Area.*

For Excel version 5.0, **First** Double-click on the chart. *If done correctly, the chart will be surrounded by a thick-striped frame.*

Select the text to be altered by clicking on it.

Type the new text in the Formula area.

Press the ENTER key. *The text should appear on the chart enclosed by handles (ie, small black squares).*

DO Exercise 5.4 - it will lead you step-by step through adding text to a chart.

Figure 5.5 This shows the text 'Northside NHS Trust Hospital' added to the chart

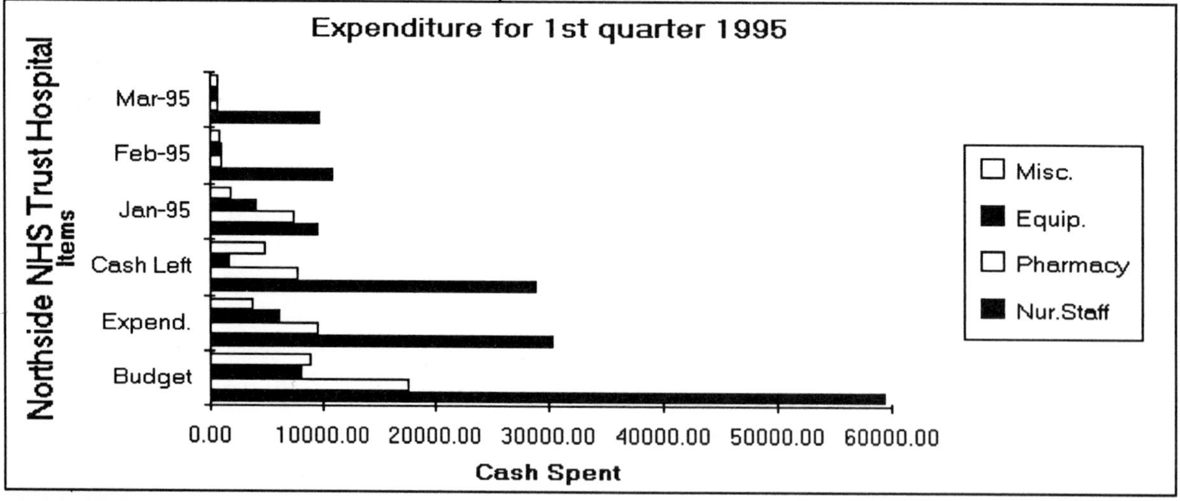

Expenditure for 1st quarter 1995

Chart — horizontal bar chart with vertical axis labelled "Northside NHS Trust Hospital" / "Items" showing Mar-95, Feb-95, Jan-95, Cash Left, Expend., Budget; horizontal axis "Cash Spent" with values 0.00, 10000.00, 20000.00, 30000.00, 40000.00, 50000.00, 60000.00; legend: Misc., Equip., Pharmacy, Nur.Staff

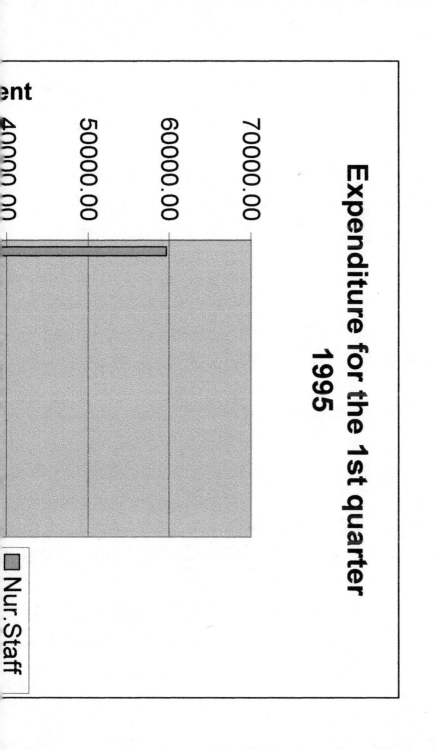

Expenditure for the 1st quarter 1995

EXERCISE 5.4 Using the worksheet **MYTASK4.XLS Chart 1**, type the title **Northside NHS Trust Hospital** and position it vertically on the chart as shown in Figure 5.5. To help you do that, follow the steps listed in FRAME 5.7.

FRAME 5.7

| | **How to add text to a chart** | ▼ | ▲ |

Remember

Adding descriptive text to a chart not only emphasises certain information, it also makes the chart easier to understand.

❶ **For Excel version 4.0:** Ensure you are in the **chart mode**. (For help, refer to FRAME 5.6, p89).
For Excel version 5.0: Double-click on the chart. *When done correctly, the chart will be surrounded by a thick striped frame.*

❷ Position the Screen pointer in the **Formula area** (see Fig. 2.3, p28) and click the left mouse button. Now, type the text, then press the ENTER key. *The Text will appear on the chart surrounded by 8 small squares called 'handles'.*

❸ Steady the Screen pointer anywhere on the text which is surrounded by small squares and press the **RIGHT** mouse button. *A command list should appear.*

❹ **For Excel version 4.0:** go to Step 5.
For Excel version 5.0: Steady the Screen pointer on the command **Format Object** and click the left mouse button. *A Format Object dialog box should appear.*

❺ Steady the Screen pointer on the command **Font** and click the left mouse button. *A dialog box should appear.*

❻ Select **size 12**, then steady the Screen pointer on the command **OK** and click the left mouse button. *The text you typed should increase in size.*

❼ **For Excel version 4.0:** Repeat **Step 3**, then jump to **Step 8**.
For Excel version 5.0: Repeat **Steps 3** and **4**, then jump to **Step 8**.

❽ **For Excel version 4.0:** Steady the Screen pointer on the command **Text** and click the left mouse button.
For Excel version 5.0: Steady the Screen pointer on the command **Alignment** and click the left mouse button. *A Text dialog box should appear.*

Fig. 5.6

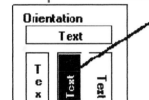

❾ Steady the Screen pointer on this box and click the left mouse button. *The box should highlight.*

❿ Steady the Screen pointer on the command **OK**, and click the left mouse button. *The Text dialog box should disappear.*
For Excel version 4.0: Steady the Screen pointer on the text. **Drag** the text and position it as shown in Figure 5.5, then steady the Screen pointer on a white area of the chart and click the left mouse button. *The handles surrounding the text should vanish.*

For Excel version 5.0: Steady the Screen pointer on the **solid border** framing the text. **Drag** the frame and position it as shown in Figure 5.5, then steady the Screen pointer on the worksheet **outside the chart** and click the left mouse button. All *the handles surrounding all the text should vanish.*

Saving an embedded chart

There are two ways to save an **embedded chart**. You can save it with the worksheet, or on its own. If you want to be able to open and print a chart without having to first open the source worksheet, then you should save the embedded chart on its own.

In Excel version 4.0, the embedded chart when saved on its own is called **Chart document**, while in Excel version 5.0 it is referred to as a **book**. The process for saving an embedded chart as a Chart document or a book vary slightly.

Read the overview below, before starting the exercise on the facing page.

OVERVIEW OF SAVING AN EMBEDDED CHART WITH A WORKSHEET

For Excel version 4.0: **Select** the 'worksheet window mode'.
(for named worksheet), **Use** the **Save** facility from the **File** menu for a named-worksheet or
(for unnamed worksheet), **Use** the **Save** or **Save As** facilities for an unnamed-worksheet.
Type an appropriate name for the worksheet.
Press the ENTER key or click on the command **OK**.

For Excel version 5.0:

(for named worksheet), **Use** the **Save** facility from the **File** menu for a named-worksheet or
(for unnamed worksheet), **Use** the **Save** or **Save As** facilities for an unnamed-worksheet.
Type an appropriate name for the worksheet.
Press the ENTER key or click on the command **OK**.

OVERVIEW OF SAVING AN EMBEDDED CHART AS A CHART DOCUMENT or BOOK

For Excel version 4.0: **Select** the 'chart window mode'.
Use the **Save As** facility.
Type an appropriate name for the 'chart document'.
Press the ENTER key or click on the command **OK**.

For Excel version 5.0: **Click** the chart once to select it.
Cut the chart using the command **Cut**.
Paste the chart on a blank worksheet using the command **Paste**.
Save the chart using the **Save As** facility.

 DO Exercise 5.5 - it will lead you step by step through the process of saving your embedded chart using both methods described above.

EXERCISE 5.5

[a] Using the steps listed in FRAME 5.8, save the embedded chart as a chart document calling it **MYCHART1**.

FRAME 5.8

| | **How to save an embedded chart as a chart document** |

❶ **For Excel version 4.0:** Ensure you are in the chart window mode then go to Step 2. (**NOTE**: *If you are in this mode you should see the word 'Chart' written after the filename on the title bar. If this is not the case, refer to FRAME 5.6, p89 for how to change to chart window mode*).

For Excel version 5.0:
(a) Click once on the worksheet **outside** the chart, then click on the chart once to select it. *When correctly selected the chart will be surrounded by a thin frame.*
(b) Position the pointer anywhere on the chart and click the **RIGHT** mouse button, then click on the command **CUT**.
(c) Click on the **new workbook** icon, then point to a cell and click the **RIGHT** mouse button.
(d) Click on the command Paste. *The chart should appear.*

❷ Now follow the steps in FRAME 2.15, p39.

Remember

1. With high speed computers the save process is fast.

2. The new workbook icon is on the Standard Toolbar and looks like this:

 EXERCISE 5.5

[b] **Users of Excel version 4.0** should ensure you are in the worksheet window mode. (*NOTE: when you are in this mode you should be able to see both the worksheet and the embedded chart. If this is not the case, refer to FRAME 5.6, p89 for how to change to worksheet window mode*).

[c] Save the worksheet under its current filename. (For help refer to FRAMES 3.16 or 3.17, p55).

[d] Close down the file (ie, the worksheet **MYTASK4**) by following the steps in FRAME 5.9 below.

FRAME 5.9

| | **How to close down a file** |

❶ Steady the Screen pointer on the command **File** and click the left mouse button. *An extended command list should appear.*

❷ Steady the Screen pointer on the command **Close** and click the left mouse button (or press the letter **C**). *The file will be closed down and a new-unnamed-blank worksheet should appear.* **N.B**: *If you have more files to close you should repeat Steps 1 and 2.*

Remember

If a **Save** dialog box appears, click on the YES button to save your work.

 EXERCISE 5.5

[e] Load the worksheet **MYTASK3**. (For help, refer to FRAME 3.10, p49).
[f] Rename the worksheet MYTASK3 and call it **MYTASK4B**, then move on. (For help, refer to FRAME 3.11, p49).

Chart document

Both Excel versions 4.0 and 5.0 allow you to create a 'chart' in a separate window instead of directly on the worksheet. There are at least two advantages with this method. You can:

- open and print the chart without having to first load or open the source worksheet;
- preserve screen space as you work on your worksheet.

When creating a 'Chart document' or a 'book', you can use data from:

- adjacent cells;
- one or more independent cells;
- range of non-adjacent cells.

For our purpose we are going to create a 'Chart' in a separate window using data from non-adjacent cells. Before starting the practice exercises on the facing page please, read the overview below as it summarises the difference in the process for version 4.0 and 5.0.

OVERVIEW OF THE STEPS FOR CREATING A CHART in a separate window using Excel version 4.0

Select the **cells** containing the data;
Select **File** on the Menu bar;
Select **New** on the extended command list.

OVERVIEW OF THE STEPS FOR CREATING A CHART in a separate window using Excel version 5.0

Select the **cells** containing the data;
Select **Insert** on the Menu bar;
Select **Chart** on the extended command list;
Select **As New Sheet** on the secondary extended command list;
Respond to the question on the ChartWizard.

 DO Exercise 5.6 - it will show you step-by-step how to create a 'chart' in a separate window using non-adjacent cells.

EXERCISE 5.6

[a] Using the worksheet **MYTASK4B,** carry out the 5-steps listed in FRAME 5.10 below remembering that:
at Step 1 you should select the cells ranging from **A6 to A9** and
at Step 2 you should select the cells ranging from **E5 to G9.**

FRAME 5.10

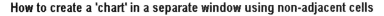

| | How to create a 'chart' in a separate window using non-adjacent cells | ▼ ▲ |

❶ Select the **first** range of cells that contain the data you want to plot,(including the the column or row labels that you want to use). *The selected cells will be highlighted.*

❷ Hold down CTRL and select the **second** range of cells. *Both the first range and the second range of cells will be highlighted.*

❸ **For Excel version 4.0:**
  (a) Steady the Screen pointer on the command **File** and click the left mouse button. *An extended list of commands should appear.*
  (b) Point to the command **New** and click the left mouse button. *A New dialog box should appear.*
  (c) Select the command **Chart**, then point and click on the command **OK.**

  For Excel version 5.0:
  (a) Steady the pointer on the command **Insert** and click the left mouse button. *An extended list of commands should appear.*
  (b) Point to the command **Chart** and click the left mouse button.
  (c) Point to the command **As New Sheet** and click the left mouse button. *A ChartWizard dialog box should appear.*
  (d) Now, follow Steps **5 to 7** in FRAME 5.1, p85.

 EXERCISE 5.6

Exercises (b-f) are for Users of Excel version 4.0 only.

[b] The chart document you have just created will be more meaningful with a legend (ie, a key identifying what each colour means). So, add a legend by following the steps listed in FRAME 5.11 below.

[c] Using all the Steps in FRAME 5.7, p91, type the title **Northside NHS Trust Hospital.**

[d] Following **only** Step 2 in FRAME 5.7, type the subtitle **Expenditure for 1st quarter 1995**

[e] Put the subtitle in a place of your choice, then remove the handles surrounding it.

FRAME 5.11 - For Users of Excel version 4.0 only

| | How to add a legend to a chart document | ▼ ▲ |

❶ Steady the Screen pointer on the command **Chart** on the **Menu bar** and click the left mouse button. *An extended list of command should appear.*

❷ Steady the Screen pointer on the command **Add Legend** and click the left mouse button (or press **L**).
*A legend should pop-up on the chart surrounded by **handles** (small back squares).*

Remember

To remove the handles surrounding a Legend or text, click outside the frame

 EXERCISE 5.6

[f] Using the steps listed in FRAME 2.15 p39, save the chart as **MYCHART2.**
[g] Print the chart using the steps listed in FRAME 4.14, p81.
[h] Using the steps in FRAME 5.9, close down the files.

Following Exercise 5.6h, you should have a clear screen. The computer RAM (Random Access Memory) should now be completely empty.

In lesson 3, it was explained that there are several terms that are used to describe the process of loading an existing document (such as a worksheet or chart) from disk into the computer RAM. These terms are Opening, Retrieving, Reading and Loading. They all mean the same thing.

It is essential to remember that:

- when you save an Embedded chart, it is stored with the worksheet as one document under one name; however:
- **For Excel version 4.0**, when you save a Chart document, the chart is saved (stored) as one document under one name and the corresponding worksheet is saved as another document under a different name in a separate file.
- **For Excel version 5.0**, when you save a Chart document, the chart is saved (stored) under its own name and the corresponding worksheet is saved with it.

This is why it is possible to open and print a chart prepared as a chart document without having to first open the source worksheet. Thus using the Chart document method, you can use the same worksheet and create different charts that can be saved under different names.

The procedure for opening a chart or its corresponding worksheet is almost the same as for any other document. The steps are listed in FRAME 3.10, p49.

Before continuing see HELP box below.

 DO Exercise 5.7 - it will show you how to open a chart and its corresponding worksheet.

For Excel version 5.0: Although a chart document is saved as a separate file, when you load that chart document, it automatically loads the corresponding worksheet. To see the worksheet, simply click on the label **Sheet1** at the **bottom left** of your Excel worksheet. To revert to the chart, click on the **Chart1** label.

For Excel version 4.0: When you load a chart document saved as a separate file, it does not automatically load the corresponding worksheet. If you require the worksheet and you are not sure of its filename, simply point to one of the bars on the column chart and click the left mouse button. A series of codes should appear in the **Formula area**. You should now be able to see the filename of the worksheet along with cells references. Using this filename you can load the worksheet.

EXERCISE 5.7

[a] Open the file called **MYCHART2** by following steps 1-5 in FRAME 3.10, p49.

[b] Read the information in the HELP box on page 96 appropriate to the Excel version you are using.

[c] If you are using **Excel version 4.0,** you should now open the worksheet **MYTASK4B** by following the steps listed in FRAME 3.10, p49 before attempting [d].

[d] Using the steps in FRAME 5.12, practise shifting between the **Worksheet window mode** and **Chart window mode** until you feel comfortable with the procedure.

FRAME 5.12

How to shift from worksheet to chart window mode and vice versa	

❶ **For Excel Version 4.0:**

(a) Steady the Screen pointer on the command **Window**, situated on the **Menu bar,** and click the left mouse button. *An extended command list should appear showing the name of your* **worksheet** *and the name of the* **Chart**.

(b) Steady the Screen pointer on the name of the required file and click the left mouse button. *The chosen file should appear.*

For Excel Version 5.0:

(a) Steady the Screen pointer on the label **Sheet1** at the bottom left of your Excel worksheet and click the left mouse button. *The corresponding worksheet should appear.*

(b) Steady the Screen pointer on the label **Chart1** at the bottom left of your Excel worksheet and click the left mouse button. *The corresponding chart should appear.*

❷ To return to the previous window **repeat** steps **a** and **b** above for the version you are using.

Remember

If a dialog box should appear asking if you want to update, respond according ie, click the **YES** or **NO** button.

ATTENTION **We have come to the end of this lesson**. Please, close down Excel, then shut down Windows following the steps listed in FRAMES 1.10 and 1.11. However, if you would like to continue straight away with the next lesson, you **must** close down Excel now, and then restart it again.

1   Charts and graphs can be created using data in your worksheet. Excel lets you create a wide variety of different types - line graphs, pie charts, bar charts etc.

2   Charts can be created directly on the worksheet using the **ChartWizard** or in a separate window.

3   Once you have created a basic chart it can be easily changed for a different type or size and updated any time. It can even be deleted using the command **Clear**.

4   Using the **Text** dialog box, labels, titles and other comments can be removed from or added to the chart as required. Legends, too, can be added or deleted at will.

5   After a chart has been created it can be saved to disk as one document with the source worksheet or it can be stored as a separate document. Either way the dynamic relationship between the chart and the source worksheet is retained. Thus whenever the data on the source worksheet is altered, the change will be reflected on the corresponding chart.

6   Excel allows you to plot charts from adjacent or non- adjacent cell ranges.

[Approximately 30-50 minutes]

NOTE: Before you start the exercises in this lesson you must have a formatted floppy disk. You can use the same disk you have been using to save files from the previous lessons. For now, **do not load any file into the computer memory until you are instructed to do so. Simply:**

■ switch on the computer and monitor now and load Windows 3.1*

■ start Excel 4.0 or 4.0a for Windows*

■ before starting any of the ensuing exercises, ensure your Sheet window and the Microsoft Excel window are merged into one (for help, refer to page 26 Fig. 2.1 and 2.2) .

*Refer to FRAMES 1.1 and 2.1 as necessary.

▬	At the end of this lesson you should be able to:	▼ ▲
EXERCISE6.1	1 Understand what is meant by a database; 2 Create a database; 3 Define the Excel database;	
EXERCISE6.2	4 Understand the rules for adding new records to Excel database; 5 Add new records to the database; 6 Find, Edit, and delete records stored in the database;	
EXERCISE6.3	7 Understand how Excel stores information in the database; 8 Sort the database using 1st and 2nd keys;	
EXERCISE6.4	9 Recall the three preliminary steps that need to be taken prior to extracting records from the database; 10 Extract records according to specific criteria;	
EXERCISE6.5	11 Copy the extracted records to a new blank worksheet; 12 Print the extracted records; 13 Save the extracted records as a separate file on disk.	

Besides being able to create worksheets and charts, Excel allows you to use the worksheet area wholly or partially to create a **database**. A database can be described as a sophisticated electronic filing cabinet capable of storing and sorting large amounts of data in an organised manner. Unlike a metal filing cabinet with lots of paper files in it, all the information in a database is saved on disk(s). All types of records about patients, staff, goods in stock can be stored in a database[1] and retrieved quickly as required.

In Excel, the database is created on a worksheet. It does not offer all the features of a special-purpose DBMS (Database Management System), such as **Paradox**[T], **FoxPro**[T] or **dBase**[T], but it can be used to:

- **Store**, for example, individual patients' records and **add** new ones;
- **Edit** or **delete** existing records;
- **Search** for specific data;
- **Sort** records in alphabetical or numerical order;
- **Extract** records meeting a specific criteria;
- **Print** records organised in a specific way.

Each column in the worksheet is used to contain one **field** (ie, one relevant piece of information like a name, or age of a patient). You can have as many fields as there are columns. The field names are located on the first row (see Fig. 6.1). Field names must be unique. They must consist of letters only, not numbers, blank cells etc, and can be up to 256 characters long.

With the exception of the first row in the worksheet, each row is used to contain one **record** (ie, details about a particular patient or staff). Although each record will have the same field, you don't need to enter data in each field.

In Excel version 4.0 the database needs to be defined before you can use special commands to help you manage your data. **In version 5.0,** you don't need to do anything special to your list of data to make it a database.

DO Exercise 6.1 - it shows you how to build a database and how to define it if you are using version 4.0.

Figure 6.1 Showing a database of *five records* with *eight fields*

	A	B	C	D	E	F	G	H	I
1	Title	Forename	Surname	Age	Sex	Status	Job	Admitted	
2	Mr	Alfred	Green	54	M	Married	Driver	12-Jul-95	
3	Mrs	Betty	White	32	F	Married	Hse wife	23-Jun-95	
4	Mrs	Carol	Grey	23	F	Married	Guide	14-Apr-95	
5	Miss	Violet	Friend	30	F	Single	Student	22-Jan-95	
6	Ms	Gay	Black	44	F	Single	Teacher	12-Jul-95	
7									

---

[1] Read Unit 3, Section 3.3 of the Chellen's User Handbook - *Information Technology for the Caring Professions,* which accompany this series. Pay particular attention to the advantages and disadvantages of a database.

EXERCISE 6.1

[a] **Using a new blank worksheet:**
- type in the eight field names shown in row 1 (refer to Figure 6.1). They are the column headings. Use the right arrow to move to the next cell across the columns.
- widen the columns where necessary (for a reminder, refer to FRAME 3.18, p57).
- centre the field names (for a reminder, refer to FRAME 4.8, p71).
- embolden the field names (for a reminder, refer to FRAME 4.3, p65).

[b] **Using the relevant skills you have learnt from previous exercises**, type the rest of the data as shown in Figure 6.1 then, save it as **MYBASE1**.

To be carried out by Users of Excel version 4.0 only
[c] Using Steps 1-4 in FRAME 6.1, define the worksheet as a database. *Doing so simplifies the searching and updating process especially when the database is extended over more columns and rows that can be seen in one screen window at a time.*

> **Remember**
>
> When you see ##### in a cell, it means the cell is too small for the number to be displayed. You can widen the column by double-clicking the right boundary of the column heading or use the Steps in FRAME 3.18, p57.

FRAME 6.1

	How to:
create a database	**define a database** [For Excel version 4.0 only]
❶ Type the field names in the first row. One field name per column. ❷ Type the records in the subsequent rows below the field names. Only one record per row.	❶ Select all the cells in the database range, including the field names and an extra blank row below the last record in the database for future expansion (refer to FRAME 2.7, p33). ❷ Select the command **Data** on the **Menu bar**. *An extended command list should appear.* ❸ Select the command **Set database** to define the database range. *When properly defined the word 'database' appears in the* **'Reference area'** *instead of the cell reference. (For a reminder of the location of the Reference area, see Fig. 2.8, p34).* ❹ Take the highlight away.

HELP	Although in Excel you can use a range of cells or the entire worksheet to create a database, do remember that the area of the worksheet used with Excel version 4.0 has to be defined whilst with version 5.0 this is not necessary.

Excel database (contd)

When creating a database it is essential to plan its structure. The information you want to keep in your database will determine the number and types of fields you should include. In Figure 6.1, p100, eight fields have been included. Of course, you can have as many fields as there are columns on the worksheet.

Excel version 4.0 Equally, when defining the area used for creating the database in version 4.0, you should always include at least one blank row in the database range. This way when you later on insert further records, they will be within the range defined and the validity of the database will be preserved saving you the trouble of having to redefine it.

RULES FOR ADDING NEW RECORDS

For Excel version 4.0, use the command **Insert** to create a blank row above the last record or if you had included a blank row in the database range as suggested above, then you can use this blank row to insert a new blank row. Otherwise you must redefine the database range to include the new records.

For Excel version 5.0, simply type the new records starting with the next blank row available on the worksheet.

or for either version, use a **data form** to add new records. Excel will add these new records to the bottom of the database and automatically extends the database range to include those new records.

Figure 6.2 The data form dialog box

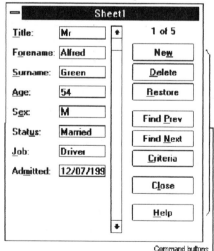

Command buttons

Editing and Formatting the Excel database

You can edit the database using any of the editing techniques you used for worksheets in Lessons 2-5, such as adding or deleting rows and columns, emboldening, aligning or copying data.

Using data form to maintain the database

The **data form** is a dialog box that provides a simple way to **view**, **change**, **add**, and **delete** records in your database, or to **find** specific records based on criteria you specify.

Excel takes the field names you set up in your database and automatically creates a Form dialog box based on those field names and provides several command buttons (Fig. 6.2) to enable you to use and maintain the database.

N.B. In Excel version 4.0, the data form displays only as many fields as will fit in the form. You cannot scroll through the data form to view the remaining fields.

 DO Exercise 6.2 - it will give you practice adding new data using **data form**.

 **EXERCISE 6.2**

Using the database you have just created carry out the following tasks by following the appropriate steps in FRAME 6.2

[a] Add three more records of your choice to the database.

[b] Find the record Mrs Grey and change it to Miss Gray.

[c] Remove from the database the three records you added in (a) above.

FRAME 6.2

How to ADD, FIND, EDIT and DELETE records using data form

❶ Ensure the worksheet containing the database is on the screen and select cell **A1**.

❷ Steady the Screen pointer on the command **Data** on the **Menu bar** and click the left mouse button. *An extended command list should appear.*

❸ Steady the Screen pointer on the command **Form** and click the left mouse button. *A dialog box should appear.*

Add new record	Find a record	Find and Edit a record	Delete a record
❹ Steady the Screen pointer on the command **New** and click the left mouse button. *Excel scrolls to the first blank record after the last nonblank record and the number indicator changes to "New record". The cursor should now be flashing in the white box next to the first field.* ❺ Type the data for the **first field**, then press the **TAB key.** *The cursor will move to the next white box ready for you to type the data for the next field.* ❻ Type the data for the remaining fields, pressing **TAB key** after each one. ❼ When you have finished entering the data for all the fields, press the ENTER key. *The New record is added to the database and another blank record is displayed.* ❽ Repeat Steps 5-7 to add further records. ❾ When you have finished adding records, steady the Screen pointer on the command **Close** and click the left mouse button.	❹ Steady the Screen pointer on the **Criteria** button and click the left mouse button. *The data form changes to accept criteria.* ❺ Type the criteria you want Excel to use when searching the database. Use the **TAB key** to move to the other white field boxes. ❻ Click on the **Find Next** button to search forward or on the **Find Prev** button to search backward. *If there is no matching records in the direction you are searching, you will hear a beep and the last matching record remains selected.* ❼ When you have finished searching, steady the Screen pointer on the command **Close** and click the left mouse button.	❹ Using Steps 4-6 for **Finding a record,** locate the record you want to edit. ❺ Steady the Screen pointer on the **white box** containing the data you want to edit and double-click the left mouse button. *The box will be highlighted.* ❻ Type the new data, then repeat Step 5 to make correction in other fields. ❼ When you have finished editing records, steady the Screen pointer on the command **Close** and click the left mouse button.	❹ Using Steps 4-6 for **Finding a record,** locate the record you want to delete. ❺ Steady the Screen pointer on the **Delete** button and click the left mouse button. A message is displayed asking for confirmation. ❻ Click on the command **OK**. *The selected record is deleted and the other records are moved up to fill the space.* ❼ Repeat the above steps to delete other records. ❽ When you have finished deleting records, steady the Screen pointer on the command **Close** and click the left mouse button.

Sorting the database

The information in the database can be organised in numerical or alphabetical order using the command **Sort**. Rows or columns can be sorted in ascending or descending order as required. The field used to sort the database is called the **Sort key**. You can specify up to three sort keys to sort a database. If you use more than one sort key (Fig. 6.3), columns or rows with the same entry for the first key are sorted according to the second and third keys. Excel uses the sort order as shown in Table 6.1 below.

Table 6.1

	for ascending order			for descending order	
1	Numbers		5	Error values	
2	Text		4	Logical values	
3	Logical values		3	Text	
4	Error values		2	Numbers	
5	Blanks		1	Blanks	
		Notice that blank cells are **always** sorted last.			

DO Exercise 6.3 - it will give you practice using the sort command.

Figure 6.3 Sort dialog box for Excel version 5.0

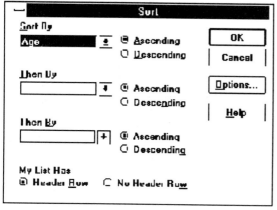

Sort dialog box for Excel version 4.0

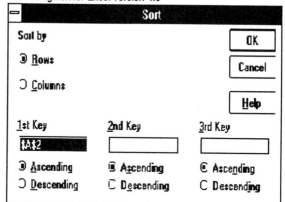

HELP

After sorting and resorting your database, you may want to return it to its original state or order. To make it easy to restore a list to a particular order, you can insert a column in which you sequentially number each row. You can use **Autofill** for that purpose. This way, later you can sort the list by that column to restore its original order.

In **Excel version 4.0**, when using sort, you should always include **all** the fields (excluding the field names) in the database ie, all columns, otherwise any fields omitted from the sort will remain in the same sequence and become attached to the wrong records.

In **Excel version 5.0**, when you select a cell and apply sort, the entire list is automatically selected.

EXERCISE 6.3

[a] Sort the database in ascending order using the field name 'age'. (**Clue**: follow the 5-steps listed in FRAME 6.3) **Note: For Users of Excel version 4.0.** at Step 1, select cells A2 to H6 and at Step 4, select the field name 'age'

[b] Sort the database in ascending order using the field names 'Surname' and 'Sex'. (**Clue**: follow the 6-steps listed in FRAME 6.3).

FRAME 6.3

	How to sort the database	

❶ For Excel version 4.0: Select the database range (**excluding** the field names). *Everything within that range will be highlighted.*
For Excel version 5.0: Select any **cell** in the list you want to sort.

❷ Select the command **Data** on the **Menu bar**. *An extended command list should appear.*

❸ Select the command **Sort**. *The Sort dialog box should appear. If necessary, steady the Screen pointer on the title bar of the dialog box and drag down so that the field names of the database are visible.*

sorting by one key

❹ For Excel version 4.0:
Move the Screen pointer onto the worksheet, steady it on the **field name** you want to sort by and click the left mouse button. *The cell is enclosed with a moving border, and a reference appears in the 1st Key box.*
For Excel version 5.0:
Type the field name you want to sort by in the **Sort By** box or use the arrow next to that box to select the field name.

❺ Click the command **OK**.
The records are sorted in a new sequence.

sorting by two keys

❹ For Excel version 4.0:
(a) Move the Screen pointer onto the worksheet, steady it on the **field name** you want to sort by and click the left mouse button. *The cell is enclosed with a moving border, and a reference appears in the 1st Key box.*
(b) Move the Screen pointer onto the **2nd key** dialog box and click the left mouse button to activate it.
(c) Move the Screen pointer onto the worksheet again, steady it on the **2nd field name** you want to sort by and click the left mouse button. *The cell is enclosed with a moving border, and a reference appears in the 2nd Key box.*
For Excel version 5.0:
(a) Type the field name you want to sort by in the **Sort By** box or use the arrow next to that box to select the field name.
(b) Move the Screen pointer onto the **1st Then By** box and click the left mouse button to activate it.
(c) Type the **2nd field name** you want to sort by or use the arrow next to that box to select the 2nd field name.

❺ Select the command **OK**.
❻ Remove the highlight.

Remember

1. If you don't like the way the data was sorted, you can use the Undo facility to undo the sort immediately.

2. For Excel version 4.0, you should not include any field names in the range of records to be sorted, otherwise they will get sorted too.

3. With Excel version 5.0, you can also sort in ascending and descending order using these icons:

Simply select any cell then click the 1st or 2nd icon.

Extracting or filtering records from a database

Once a database gets to a certain length, it may be useful to select certain records and copy them to another part of the worksheet for closer examination or to obtain a print out. The procedure for obtain a sublist of records from the database is different depending on which version of Excel you are using, 4.0 or 5.0.

In **Excel version 4.0**, the sublist of records required must be extracted from the entire list and placed on another area of the worksheet.

In **Excel version 5.0**, the sublist of records required is filtered from the entire list and displayed on the screen.

In either version, using the commands **Copy** and **Paste** or **Cut** and **Paste**, the extracted records or the filtered list of records can then be copied to another worksheet for further analysis.

DO Exercise 6.4 - it will show you how to extract or filter records from the database, using the sample database you created in Exercise 6.1

Figure 6.4

	A	B	C	D	E	F	G	H	I
1	Title	Forename	Surname	Age	Sex	Status	Job	Admitted	
2	Mr	Alfred	Green	54	M	Married	Driver	12-Jul-95	
3	Mrs	Betty	White	32	F	Married	Hse wife	23-Jun-95	
4	Mrs	Carol	Grey	23	F	Married	Guide	14-Apr-95	
5	Miss	Violet	Friend	30	F	Single	Student	22-Jan-95	
6	Ms	Gay	Black	44	F	Single	Teacher	12-Jul-95	
∪									
12									
13	Title	Forename	Surname	Age	Sex	Status	Job	Admitted	
14									
15									
16	Title	Forename	Surname	Age	Sex	Status	Job	Admitted	
17									

EXERCISE 6.4 Using the sample database in Figure 6.1 (which you should have on your screen) we are going to practise extracting records from it.

We are going to use a criterion that finds records of all patients who are 'single'.

Simply follow the steps and sub-steps listed in the FRAME 6.4 below.

FRAME 6.4a - For Excel version 4.0 only

How to extract records

❶ Redefine the database.
1. Make sure the worksheet containing the database is on the screen.
2. Carry out the 4-steps in Frame 6.1, p101.
3. Select **row 1** which should contain the field names.
4. Using the command **Copy** and **Paste** (see FRAME 3.8, p47) copy the field names and paste them in **row 13** and in **row 16**.
5. *Your worksheet should now resemble that of Fig.6.4.*

Specify the Criteria.
1. Select cell range **A13 to H14**. *The selected cells should now be highlighted.*
2. Steady the Screen pointer on the command **Data**, located on the **Menu bar**, and click the left mouse button. *An extended command list should appear.*
3. Select the command **Set Criteria**.

Define the Extract Range.
1. Select cells **A16 to H16**.
2. Steady the Screen pointer on the command **Data**, located on the **Menu bar**, and click the left mouse button. *An extended command list should appear.*
3. Select the command **Set Extract**.

Extract selected records
1. Select cell **F14** and type the criterion **Single**, then press RETURN.
2. Select **Data** on the **Menu bar**.
3. Select the command **Extract**.
4. *A dialog box should appear offering the choice to extract unique records only. This allows you to eliminate any duplicate records from the selection.*
5. Select the command **OK**.
   All the records matching the search criterion are extracted and copied below the extract range.

FRAME 6.4b - For Excel version 5.0 only

How to filter records

❶ Make sure the worksheet containing the database is on the screen.

Select a cell containing data.

Steady the Screen pointer on the command **Data**, located on the **Menu bar** and click the left mouse button. *An extended command list should appear.*

Point to the command **Filter** and click the left mouse button. *Another extended command list should appear.*

Point to the command **Autofilter**. *Drop down arrows should appear next to each column label in the database.*

❻ Move your pointer onto the arrow in the column containing the data you want to filter and click the left mouse button. *A drop down list should appear.*

❼ Point to the item/criteria you want to use and click the left mouse button. *Only the records meeting the criteria are displayed, the rest of the rows are hidden. **Notice the arrow you clicked in Step 6 has changed colour.***

❽ To filter the list further using other criteria, repeat **Steps 6 and 7**. *The list is further reduced according to the additional criteria.*

Note:
- If you want to go back a step and reselect under another criteria, point to the coloured arrow again and click the left mouse button. Then point to the criteria **ALL** (you may need to scroll the list upwards to see it) and click the left mouse button.
- When you are ready to return to the main list in the database, remove the drop down arrows next to each column label by repeating Steps 3,4 and 5 in FRAME 6.4b above.
- If you want to save or print an 'extract' follow the appropriate steps in FRAME 6.5, p109.

Printing and Saving your extracts

Once you have extracted or filtered a set of records, it can be printed onto paper and saved to disk as a separate file if you so wish. The procedure for doing these is slightly different depending on which version of Excel you are using, 4.0 or 5.0. The ensuing exercise will show you the technique.

DO Exercise 6.5 - it will lead you step by step through the process of saving and printing the records you have extracted in the previous exercise.

Figure 6.5 Screen showing the extracted or filtered records only

	A	B	C	D	E	F	G	H	I
1	Title	Forename	Surname	Age	Sex	Status	Job	Admitted	
2	Miss	Violet	Friend	30	F	Single	Student	22-Jan-95	
3	Ms	Gay	Black	44	F	Single	Teacher	12-Jul-95	
4									
5									

Figure 6.6 Utility toolbar for Excel version 4.0

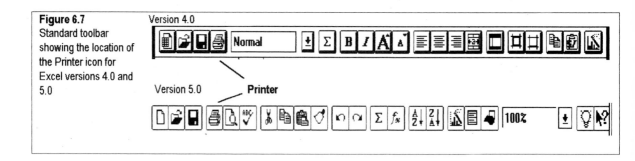

Set Print Area

Figure 6.7
Standard toolbar
showing the location of
the Printer icon for
Excel versions 4.0 and
5.0

Version 4.0

Version 5.0   Printer

EXERCISE 6.5

Assuming you still have your extracted records on the screen, you may want to print them on their own or save them to disk.

Using the steps listed in FRAME 6.5 below, do the following:

[a] Print the records you have extracted - including the field names. (Users of Excel version 4.0 should select those records which appear beneath the field names in row 16).

[b] Save the records you have extracted to disk.

[c] Close the file containing the records you have extracted.

FRAME 6.5

| How to | | Remember |

Print only

❶ **For Excel version 5.0:** Go to Step 2.
For Excel version 4.0:
(a) Ensure that the Utility Toolbar Fig. 6.6 is switched on. (For Help refer to FRAME 2.3, p29).
(b) Select the area of the worksheet which contains the extracted records, including the field names. *When properly selected the area should be highlighted.*

❷ Ensure the printer is ready for use.

❸ **For Excel version 5.0:** Go to Step 4.
For Excel version 4.0: click on the **Set Printer Area** icon located on the Utility toolbar (see Fig.6.5).

The message Print Area will appear in the Reference Area (Fig.2.8, p34).

❹ Now, click on the **Printer** icon on the **Standard Toolbar**.

Save to disk and/or Print

❶ Select the area of the worksheet which contains the extracted/filtered records, including the field names. *When properly selected the area should be highlighted.*

❷ Steady the pointer on one of the highlighted cells and click the RIGHT mouse button. *An extended command list should appear.*

❸ Click on the command **Copy**.
A marquee should surround the area selected.

❹ Click on the **New worksheet** icon situated on the Toolbar. *A fresh worksheet should appear.*

❺ Click on the command **Edit** on the **Menu bar**. *An Extended command list should appear.*

❻ Click on the command **Paste**. *The extracted records should be appear on the worksheet as shown in Fig. 6.5.*

❼ **To save:** Follow the steps listed in FRAME 2.15, p39
To print: Follow the steps listed in FRAME 4.14, p81

---

1. A **Marquee** is a moving border surrounding an area that has been selected for copying.

New worksheet Icons

4.0   5.0

2. You can position the Utility Toolbar anywhere on the screen

---

HELP

- **To return to the database after you have carried out Steps 1-7:**
  Click on the command **File** on the Menu bar then, click on the command **Close**. If a dialog box should appear respond accordingly.
- When closing down your database following the activity of extracting records, a dialog box will appear asking if you want to save changes. You should click on the **NO** button.

ATTENTION   **We have come to the end of this lesson and this tutorial.** We hope you have found this workbook useful.

Please, close down Excel, then shut down Windows following the steps listed in FRAMES 1.10 and 1.11.

APPENDIX 1- Steps for formatting a disk using Windows Utility program

A floppy or hard disk must be prepared (formatted) before information can be recorded onto it. A formatting program is used for this purpose. If you are using a system with a hard disk, the formatting program is usually on it. Otherwise you will need to load it into the computer. Before you start formatting a disk it is important to bear the following points in mind:

Aim: To format 3.5" &/or 5.25" floppy disks using Windows *Safe Format* procedure on a computer with a hard disk.

Equipment required:
1. An IBM or IBM compatible computer with a hard disk and ONE or TWO **High Density** drives - one being 3.5" and the other being 5.25".
2. Floppy disk(s) to be formatted.

Procedure:
- Run Windows.
- When the Windows Program Manager appears, insert your disk to be formatted into the appropriate drive with the label facing upwards and towards you.
- From the Windows Program Manager open the Main Program group if it is closed by double-clicking on the icon, then double-click on the **File Manager** Icon.
- Click once on **Disk** on the File Manager Menu Bar.
- When a drop-down menu appears, click once on **Format Disk,** the Format Disk dialogue box illustrated below will appear. Now follow the six instructions below.

Figure A1.1

❶ Place the cursor in the 'Label' box and click once then type a name to label your disk, for example, MYWORKDISK.

❷ If you want to format your disk at 720K or 360K, then click once on the down arrow in the 'Capacity' box, for an extended list, and click once on 720K or 360K.

❸ If you want to format your disk in drive B, then click once on the down arrow in the 'Disk In' box and click once on drive B.

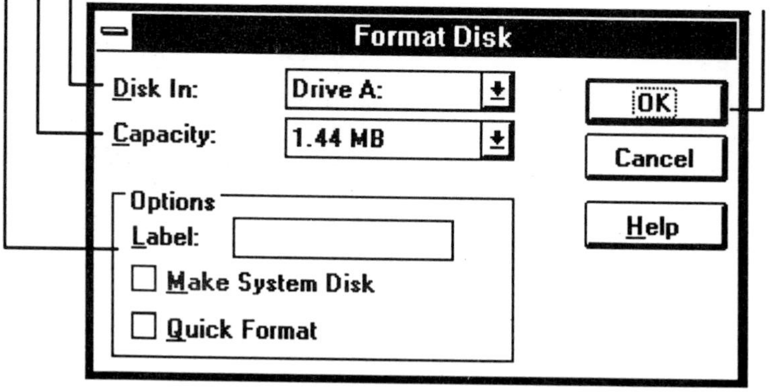

❹ Click once on OK

❺ When the confirmation box appears choose YES to start the formatting process.

❻ When the disk is formatted you will be asked if you want to format another disk. Respond accordingly by clicking on the YES or NO button.

110

APPENDIX 2

When Excel is started, only the **Standard toolbar** may be displayed initially. It contains the most frequently used tools. However, there are a further toolbars that can be displayed. All the toolbars can be displayed and can be positioned anywhere on the screen. For information about displaying toolbars see FRAME 2.3, p29. The shape of the toolbars can also be changed. Excel retains the position and shape of displayed toolbars until you change them. In this workbook we are going to look at the following four toolbars: **Formatting, Chart, Drawing** and **Utility** for both Excel versions 4.0 and 5.0

Additional Toolbars for Excel version 5.0

Figure A2.1 - Formatting toolbar

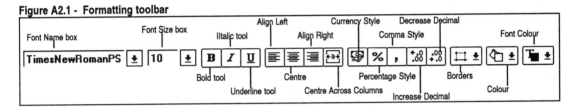

Figure A2.2 - Chart toolbar

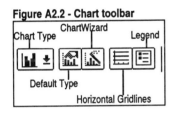

Figure A2.3 - Drawing toolbar

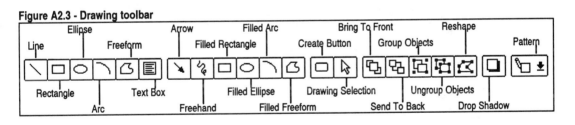

Figure A2.4 - Custom Utility toolbar

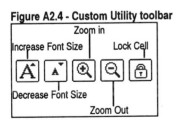

Additional Toolbars for Excel version 4.0

Fig. A2.1 Formatting toolbar

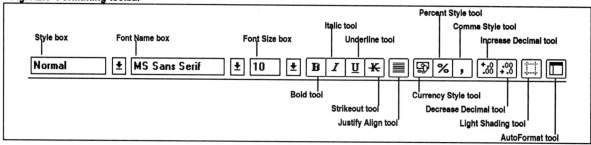

Fig. A2.2 Chart toolbar

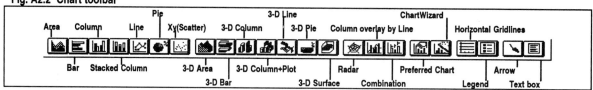

Fig. A2.3 Drawing toolbar

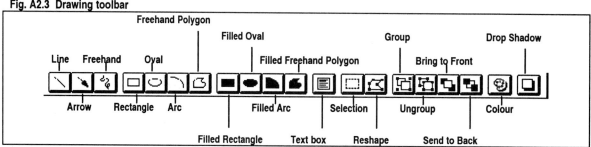

Fig. A2.4 Utility toolbar

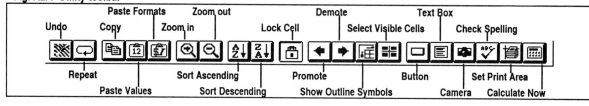

112

DESCRIPTION OF THE TOOLS ON THE

Formatting Toolbar
(Fig. A2.1)

Allows you to:

Style box	apply different styles to cell.
Font Name box	apply fonts of your own choosing.
Font Size box	apply the font size you want.
Bold	apply **bold** to text.
Italic	apply *italic* to text.
Underline	apply underline to text.
Strikeout	draw a line through text.
Justify Align	line the text against the left and right sides of cells or text boxes.
Currency Style	apply the currency style to chosen cells.
Percent Style	apply the % style to chosen cells.
Comma Style	apply the comma style to chosen cells.
Increase Decimal	display an additional decimal place each time you click the tool.
Decrease Decimal	display one less decimal place each time you click the tool.
Light Shading	apply a light shading pattern to the chosen cells, graphic objects or chart items.
AutoFormat	apply the last table format applied with the AutoFormat command.
Align Left	line the text against the left side of the cells or text boxes.
Centre	centre the text in cells, text boxes etc.
Align Right	Line the text against the right side of the cells or text boxes.
Centre Across-Columns	centre the text across several columns.
Borders	apply borders to selected cell or cells.
Colour	apply colour to the selected cell or cells.
Font Colour	apply colour to the selected text.

Chart Toolbar
(Fig. A2.2)

Allows you to:

Area	create a simple area chart.
Bar	create a simple bar chart.
Column	create a simple column chart.
Stacked column	create a stacked column chart.
Line	create a line chart.
Pie	create a pie chart.
Xy(Scatter)	create an Xy(scatter) chart.
3-D Area	create a 3-D area chart.
3-D Bar	create a 3-D bar chart.
3-D Column	create a 3-D column chart.
3-D Column + Plot	create a 3-D column with a 3-D plot area chart.
3-D Line	create a 3-D line or ribbon chart.
3-D Pie	create a 3-D pie chart with value labels as percentages.
3-D Surface	create a 3-D surface chart.
Radar	create a Radar chart.
Column and Line	create a combination of a column and a line chart.
Combination	create a combination of a column and line chart containing three data series.
Preferred/Default type	draw a chart in the preferred format.
ChartWizard	create and embedded chart.
Horizontal Gridlines	add or delete major gridlines.
Legend	add or delete chart legend.
Arrow	add an arrow to a chart document.
Text box	add an unattached text item to a chart.
Chart Type	change the chart type of the active chart or selected data series.

Drawing Toolbar
(Fig. A2.3)

Allows you to use a cross-hair pointer to

Line	draw a straight line.
Arrow	draw an arrow on the worksheet or add an arrow to a chart.
Freehand	draw a continuous freehand line.
Rectangle	draw a rectangle or square.
Oval/Elipse	draw an oval or circle.
Arc	draw and arc or a circle segment.
Freeform/hand	draw different shapes.
Filled Rectangle	draw a rectangle or square filled with background colour or pattern.
Filled Oval/Elipse	draw an oval or circle filled with background colour or pattern.
Filled Arc	draw an arc or circle segment filled with background colour or pattern.
Filled Freeform/hand	draw freehand polygon filled with background colour or pattern.
Text box	draw a text box in which you can type.
Selection	select graphic objects.
Reshape	change the shape of a polygon.
Group	join various objects into one.
Ungroup	separate group objects into individual ones.
Bring to Front	place selected objects in front of others.
Send to Back	place selected objects behind others.
Colour	change the foreground colour of chosen cells.
Drop Shadow	add a shadowed rectangle around the cells.
Create button	drag a document to create a button.
Pattern	apply patterns to the selection.

Utility Toolbar
(Fig. A2.4)

Allows you to:

Undo	undo the last action or command.
Repeat	repeat the last action or command.
Paste Values	paste only the values from the copied cells into the paste area.
Zoom In	magnify the document.
Zoom Out	display the document at a lower size.
Sort Ascending	sort chosen rows in ascending order.
Sort Descending	sort chosen rows in descending order.
Lock Cell	lock chosen cells to prevent changes being made to them). Also unlock them.
Promote	assign the chosen columns or rows to one level higher.
Demote	assign the chosen columns or rows to one level lower.
Show Outline Symbols	display or hide the symbols on a worksheet.
Select Visible Cells	select only visible cells in a selection.
Button	use a cross-hair pointer to draw a button.
Text box	draw a text box in which you can type.
Camera	copy a picture of the chosen cells.
Check Spelling	spell check a worksheet.
Set Print Area	select the range of cells for printing.
Calculate Now	calculate the formulas in a document.
Increase Font Size	increase the font size of selected text.
Decrease Font Size	decrease the font size of selected text.

APPENDIX 3:

How to create a custom toolbar and add icons/buttons to it.
(For Version 5.0)
[Follow the 3 Phases in sequence]

Phase 1 - Creating the custom toolbar

1 Steady the pointer on the command **View** on the Menu bar and click the left mouse button. *A drop down menu should appear.*
2 Position the pointer on the command **Toolbars** and click the left mouse button. *A toolbar dialog box should appear.*
3 Steady the pointer in the box labelled **Toolbar name** and double-click the left mouse button. *Its contents should highlight.*
4 Now type : **Utility**
5 Click on the command **Customize.** *A small rectangular box - your custom toolbar, should appear on your worksheet usually beneath the Reference area box. Also a Customize dialog box should appear.*

Phase 2 - Adding buttons or icons to the custom toolbar.

1 Steady the pointer on the command **Text Formatting** in the box labelled **Categories** and click the left mouse button. *A range of buttons ie, icons should appear underneath the Buttons box.*

2 Steady the pointer on the $\boxed{A}$ **Large A** icon and drag it from the Buttons box and position it in the custom toolbar you created in Step 5 in Phase 1 above. *The button/icon you dragged should now appear on that custom toolbar.*

3 Steady the pointer on the $\boxed{A}$ **Small A** icon and drag it from the **Buttons** box and position it in the **custom toolbar** next to the Large A icon. *Now you should have 2 buttons in your custom toolbar and its title 'Utility' should be clearly visible.*

4 Move your pointer to the box labelled **Categories**, and click on the command **Utility**. *A different range of button should appear.*

5 Drag the $\boxed{\oplus}$ **Increased magnification** icon and place it next to the second icon on the your custom toolbar.

6 Drag the _____ **Decreased magnification** icon and place it next to the third icon on your custom toolbar.

7 Drag the $\boxed{🔒}$ **Lock** icon and position it next to the fourth icon on your custom toolbar.

8 Click on the command **Close** located on the Customize dialog box. *You should now have **five** icons on your custom toolbar. (You can add others as and when required).*

Phase 3 - Positioning your custom toolbar next to the other toolbars on your worksheet.

1 Steady the pointer on the title 'Utility' of your **custom toolbar**, double-click the left mouse button **or** drag and position it on the **Reference area** box. *As you release the mouse button the toolbar will be fixed underneath the other toolbars. Your custom toolbar can be switched ON and OFF just like the others.*

114

APPENDIX 4

TROUBLESHOOTING

Problem	Action
1. My document/worksheet is not printing.	• Check that the printer is properly connected with the computer and it is on line. • Check that the printer cartridge is not empty or missing. • Check that the printer has not run out of paper or jammed. • Be patient if you are using a network or your document contains complicated graphics.
2. I have pressed the wrong key or touch the mouse button by mistake and now there is a dialog box on the screen in the middle of my worksheet.	• Press the ESCape key on the keyboard. • Click the Cancel button on the dialog box. • Use the Undo facility immediately.
3. I have clicked on the wrong command or menu title.	• Use the Undo facility immediately. • Click on the title bar.
4. I have minimised the worksheet window by mistake.	• Look for the minimised icon at the bottom of your screen and double click on it. (**Remember**, sometimes you may need to close down other windows to uncover the icon).
5. My computer is not responding to any commands.	• Press the ESCape key, then try again. • Try saving your work. • Switch off the machine and start again.
6. The computer is not saving my document to my floppy, and there is no error message.	• Check that you have selected the correct drive. • Check that the disk in not write-protected. • Try another disk as the one you are using might be faulty. • Ensure you are using a formatted disk. • Ensure the filename is not more than 7 characters long and you have not included unwanted spaces or used comma instead of fullstop. • Try saving the material to your hard disk.
7. The worksheet has moved to the right or to the left of the screen.	• Use the scroll button to make required adjustment.
8. The worksheet window is not occupying the full screen.	• Click on the Maximise button.
9. I have deleted the wrong cell.	• Use the Undo facility immediately.
10. While doing the exercises in this workbook, I have spoilt the worksheet I am working with.	• Load a fresh copy your floppy, if there is one available. Otherwise close the spoilt worksheet without saving it and start with a fresh one.
11. While working through the exercises in this workbook, I pressed a key or clicked an icon as instructed, but nothing happened.	• Try pressing the suggested key or clicking the suggested icon again. • Ensure that you are pressing the correct button on the mouse or on the keyboard.
12. The Screen pointer assumes an unexpected shape.	• Press the ESCape key on the keyboard. • Move the Pointer in the middle of the worksheet and click the left mouse button.
13. A command on the menu list is not responding and it is light grey instead of black.	• Read the instructions in the workbook again. • Ensure you have selected the cell correctly and then try activating the command again.
14. The computer beeps every time I try to carry out a particular procedure.	• Read the instructions again as you are doing something illegal.
15. I click on an icon and it does not respond.	• Ensure the **tip** of your pointer is on the icon and try again. • Ensure you are using the correct number of clicks ie, one click or double-click. If you are using double-click, ensure you are doing so correctly. • Ensure you are press the correct mouse button.
16. A dialog box pops up unexpectedly.	• Press the ESCape key on the keyboard or click on the Cancel button on the dialog box.
17. The computer is beeping for no apparent reason.	• Check that nothing is inadvertently resting on the keyboard.

APPENDIX 5

Assignment: A Sample Electronic Duty Sheet

1 Now it is time to test the skills that you have acquired so far.

2 We are going to create a very different type of spreadsheet which deals with helping Nurse Managers with the preparation of Staff Duty Rota.

3 The finished product will look like Figure A5.1 below.

4 Please do not attempt to **simply** copy out the Duty Sheet shown in the Figure A5.1 as some of the numeric data in the cells are processed by the computer and not by you. To help you reproduce the Electronic Duty Sheet, please follow the steps on the next page.

5 When following the steps, please make sure that you select the correct cell or cells as instructed. If you make a mistake, use the editing skills you have acquired to rectify the situation.

6 After you have constructed the Electronic sheet, some cells will have been protected so that you cannot accidentally overwrite their contents.

Figure A5.1

	SAT.			SUN.			MON.			TUES.			WED.			THUR.			FRI.		
NAME OF STAFF	E	L	N	E	L	N	E	L	N	E	L	N	E	L	N	E	L	N	E	L	N
	0	0	0	0	0	0	0	0	0	0	0	0	0	0	0	0	0	0	0	0	0
W/M Black							1			1			1			1			1		
D/W/M White	1						1			1			1			1			SD		
S/N Grey		1		1									1			1			TO		
S/N Brown		1		1				1						1			1		1		
S/N Orange	1			1				1		1									1		
E/N Violet		SD			1		1				1		1								
E/N Playsafe		1			1		1				1						1				
N/A Drinkwater	1			1				1									1		SD		
N/A Allcock		1		1									1			1			1		
N/A Giveway										A	N	N	U	A	L		L	E	A	V	E
N/A Woodhouse							1			1			1			1			SD		
E/N Sleeptight														1			1				1
S/N Nightnurse		1			1			1			1										
TOTAL STAFF am SHIFT	3			4			4			3			2			3			1		
TOTAL STAFF pm SHIFT		4			3			3			3			4			4			4	
TOTAL STAFF night SHIFT			1			1			1			1			1			1			1

Keys: SD = Study day; TO = Time owing; E = Early Shift; L = Late Shift; N= Night Shift

Instructions for using the Sample Electronic Duty Sheet: Simply type the name of the staff and **use the four Arrow keys** to move to an empty cell, where you should type a 1 to indicate whether the staff is on Early, Late or Night shift for each day of the week. You can type words or sentences to indicate annual leave, study days and so on, **one letter in each cell.** The two days off are already mapped by the shaded area. When you try to enter data in a cell which is protected, a dialog box will appear. You should click on **OK** to continue. Now, experiment with your duty sheet. DO NOT forget to save your work.

Creating an Electronic Duty Sheet.

[Follow the 8 Phases in sequence]

Column centred icon	Text centred icon	Decrease Magnification or Zoom Out icon	SUM icon	Lock Cell icon

Phase 1 -
1. Start Excel
2. Ensure your Sheet window and the Microsoft window are merged into one. (For help, refer to page 26 Fig. 2.1 & 2.2).
3. Ensure the FORMATTING and UTILITY Toolbar s are switched on. (For help, refer to Appendix 2, Fig.A2.4).
4. Click on the **Select All** button (see Fig. 2.6, p32).
5. Change the point size to **9** or **10** and the Font to **MS Serif**.
6. Narrow the width of column **B** to **V** to 2.86cm. (For help, use Method 4, FRAME 3.18, p57).

Phase 2 - DAYS OF THE WEEK
1. Select cell **B4** and type **SAT.**   (including the fullstop)
2. Select cell **E4** and type **SUN.**
3. Select cell **H4** and type **MON.**
4. Select cell **K4** and type **TUE.**
5. Select cell **N4** and type **WED.**
6. Select cell **Q4** and type **THU.**
7. Select cell **T4** and type **FRI.**
8. Select cell range **B4** to **V4** and click on the **Column centred** icon .

Phase 3 - CODE FOR EARLY, LATE, NIGHT shifts
1. Select cell **B5** and type **E**
2. Select cell **C5** and type **L**
3. Select cell **D5** and type **N**
4. Select cell range **B5** to **D5**, click on the **Text centred icon then** drag the **Fill-handle** to cell **V5.**
5. Select cell **B6** and type the figure **0**
6. Ensure cell **B6** is still selected, click the **Text centred** icon **and then drag** the **Fill-handle** to cell **V6.**
7. Select cell range **A1** to **V6**, then click on the **Bold** icon
8. Remove the highlight
9. Click on the **Zoom Out** icon.

Phase 4 - LABELS AND CALCULATION FORMULAE
1. Select cell **A20** and type **TOTAL STAFF am SHIFT**
2. Select cell **A21** and type **TOTAL STAFF pm SHIFT**
3. Select cell **A22** and type **TOTAL STAFF night SHIFT**
4. Select cell range **A20** to **V22** and click on the **Bold** icon.
5. Enlarge the width of **column A** for **Best fit (Autofit)**. (For help, refer to FRAME 3.18, p57 Method 1).
6. Make sure row 6 is in view, then select cell **B20** and click on the **SUM** icon on the Standard Toolbar, **then** press the ENTER key.
7. Select cell **C21** and click on the **SUM** icon, then press ENTER.
8. Select cell **D22** and click on the **SUM** icon, then press ENTER.
9. Repeat this pattern with the subsequent columns for the remaining days of the week.

Phase 5 - PATTERNS FOR DAYS OFF
1. Select cell range **B7** to **G7**.
2. Steady the pointer on any one of the darkened cells and click the **RIGHT** mouse button to reveal a command list.
3. **For Excel version 4.0**:
   (a) Click on the command **Patterns**.
   (b) Point to the word **automatic** in the **Foreground box** and click the left mouse button.

For Excel version 5.0:
   (a) Click on the command **Format Cells**.
   (b) Click on the command **Patterns**.
4. Point to the **red rectangle/square** and click the left mouse button.
5. Click on the command **OK**, then remove the highlight.
6. Use the command **Copy** and **Paste** (see FRAMES 3.9 & 3.8, p47) and reproduce the Z-like pattern in Figure A5.1
N.B. *If you have difficulty putting pattern for cell range T19-V19. The simplest solution is to copy and paste cell range T12 to V12*

Phase 6 - TITLES AND SUBTITLES
1. Select cell **A6**, click on the **Text Centred** icon and then type: **NAME OF STAFF**.
2. Select cell **A1** and type: **Northside NHS Trust Hospital**
3. Select cell **A2** and type: **Princess Diana Unit**.
4. Select cell **A3** and type: **Weekly Duty Sheet, Week Commencing:**
5. Select cell **J3** and type **12.12.95**
6. Select cell range **A1** to **V2** and click on the **column centred** icon .

Phase 7 - BORDERS AND GRIDS
1. Select cell range **A7** to **A19** and put a border. (For help, refer to FRAME 4.11, p75.)
2. Select cell range **B4** to **V22**.
3. Follow Steps **2** to **7** in FRAME 4.11, p75 column 1, **BUT** when you reach the **7th Step**, before choosing **OK**, click on the **left**, **right**, **top** , and **bottom** boxes first.
4. Select cell range **B7** to **V22** and click the **Text centred** icon.

Phase 8 - PROTECTING SOME CELLS
1. Select cell range **A7** to **V19** and click on the depressed grey **Lock Cell** icon on the Utility Toolbar. It will pop out and become dark.
2. Select cell **J3** and click on the **Lock Cell** icon.
3. **For Excel version 4.0:** Select the command **Options** on the **Menu bar** to reveal an extended list.
   For Excel version 5.0: Select the command Tools on the Menu bar to reveal an extended list.
4. **For Excel version 4.0:** From the extended list click on the command **Protect document**.
   For Excel version 5.0: Select the command **Protection**, then the command **Protect Sheet**.
5. Click on **OK** on the Dialog box (Do not enter a password).
6. Repeat Step 3.
7. **For Excel version 4.0:** click on the command **Display**.
   For Excel version 5.0: click on the command **Options**
8. Click on the command **Gridlines** on the Dialog box.
9. Click on the command **OK**, then click on cell **A2**.

WELL DONE! Your Electronic Duty Sheet is now ready for use. See instructions on page 116 below Figure A5.1.
HELP. If after you have completed all the steps in phase 8, you then discover an error that needs to be altered, you must first unprotect the worksheet by selecting the command **Options/Tools** on the Menu bar and clicking the command **Unprotect document**. When you've finished your alterations, repeat Steps **3-5** of phase **8**.

INDEX

Aligning
  text across columns, 71
  text in cell(s), 71
  methods of, 70
Altering
  fonts, 66, 68, 69
  point sizes, 66, 68, 69
Analysis ToolPak, 24
Application, 10, 13
  working with, 14
Applying formula to figures, 61
Autofill, 24

Backspace key, 6, 35, 40
Blank worksheet, 40
Bold, 64, 65
Borders, 74
  put around an area, 75
Button, 13

Calculations, 82
Cells - vertical text, 24
Centring
  text across columns, 24,71
  text in cell(s), 71
Changing
  charts and graphs, 98
  contents of cells, 36
  appearance of data, 64
  window mode, 88
Chart, 24, 82, 85
  Adding descriptive text to, 90,91
  document, 94
  toolbar, 112
  window mode, 88
  Wizard, 24, 84, 85
  to represent data, 84
  Updating, relocating , 87
Clicking, 3,15
Closing down
  a file, 93
  applications, 19
Columns, 50, 51,52,53
Column width
  adjusting, 56, 57
  decreasing, 58
  increasing, 58
Commands, 4
  Clear and delete, 44
  to insert bold/italic, 65
  Save As... , 58
  editing, 44
Computer, 8, 9
Copy and paste, 46, 47
Copying
  a document from disk, 58
  data, 24
Creating
  a 'Chart document', 94, 95
  a database, 101
  a new chart, 85
  data series, 42
Crosstab ReportWizard, 24
Ctrl key, 6
Currency symbols, 82
Cursor, 5, 6
Cut and paste, 46, 47

Data, 42
  series, 42
  Presentation of, 82, 84
  form, 102
  entry, 34, 35, 40, 82
Database,103,106
  adding new records, 102
  sorting, 104, 105
  extracting records, 106
Delete
  a chart, 87
  cell(s), 52
  rows, 50,51,52,53
  columns, 50,51,52,53
  text, 36, 37, 40
Deselect, 33
Dialog box ,18
Disk, 110
DOS C:\> prompt, 9
Double-clicking, 3
Double-headed arrow, 5
Dragging, 3, 85
Drawing toolbar, 112

Errors, correcting, 40
Editing
  Excel database, 102
  an embedded chart, 86
  data in cells, 40, 44, 45, 46
Embedded chart, 84, 87,88
ESCape key, 6
Excel, 3, 8
  on the network, 25
Excel
  database, 100, 102
  for Windows, 2, 24
  Print Preview window, 78
  program icon, 25
  window, 40
  worksheet, 26, 28, 30
Export facilities, 24
Extended-menu list, 29

Field names, 107
File extension, 49
Filename, 49
Fonts, 66, 67, 68, 69
Font size, 67
  decrease, 67
  increasing, 67
Formatting
  data in your worksheet, 72
  Excel database, 102
  toolbar, 112
  a disk, 110, 111
Formula, 1, 61
  area, 5

Graphs, 24
Gridlines, 74, 75
  hiding, 75

Import facilities, 24
Input, 46
Inserting
  borders, 74
  gridlines, 74, 75
  rows. 50, 51,52,53

  columns, 50, 51,52,53
  shade, 74
  text, 36, 37
Insertion point, 36

Keyboard, 4, 40

Loading
  a worksheet from disk, 48
  Excel, 28
  Windows, 9

Macro, 24
Maintaining a database, 103
Menu bar, 18, 22
Menus, 18
Minimize button , 15
Monitor switches, 9
Mouse, 3
  basic techniques, 22
  button , 3, 11, 29
Move around various parts of the
worksheet, 3
Moving data, 24, 42, 43, 46
  drag technique, 42

Naming a worksheet, 38, 40
New worksheet, 40
Num Lock, 6
Numeric values. 71
  displayed, 72

Opening
  an existing chart, 96, 97
  menus, 19

Pointing,3
Power failure, 40
Preview a worksheet, 78, 79, 81
Printing, 79, 80, 81, 82
  dialog box, 80
  extracts, 108, 109
Program, 22
  group icon, 22
  groups, 12, 13
  manager, 10, 22
Putting cell entries in
  bold, 65
  italics, 65

Quick Reference Guide, 114

Reading a file from disk, 48
Removing the handles
  surrounding a Legend, 95
  surrounding text, 95
Removing unwanted data, 58
Renaming a document/file, 48
Resizing
  a window. 5,17
  an embedded chart, 89
Restore deleted data, 45
Retrieve a file from other drives.
48, 49
Return key, 6
Reversing unwanted deletion, 58
Right mouse button , 51
Rows, 50, 51,52,53

Save
  dialog box, 19, 93

  to drive A, 40, 55, 58
  a named document, 54, 55
  a new worksheet, 38
  an embedded chart, 92, 93
  your extracts, 108, 109
Screen, 22
Screen pointer, 5, 6, 11, 36, 43,
  looks like, 33
Scrolling the worksheet, 31
Select
  a range of cells, 75
  an embedded chart, 89
  a row, 33
  a column, 33
  cells, 32,33
Shade, 74
  an area, 75
  shading, 74
Shift between chart and
worksheet, 89, 97
Spacebar, 40
Speeding data entry, 58
Spellchecker, 24, 77
  overview, 76
  dialog box, 76
Spreadsheet
  uses & advantages, 1,2
SUM function, 82
Switching ON and OFF
  a computer with Windows
installed, 8, 20
  additional Toolbars, 29

TAB key, 6, 31
Temporary
  files, 22
  memory, 46
Text, 36, 37
Title bar, 38
Toolbars, 28, 29,113
Troubleshooting, 115
Typing Functions or Formulae, 63

Undo
  facility, 58,107
  a change. 51,57
Utility Toolbar, 109, 112

Windows, 10, 14, 22
  maximizing, 15, 27
  minimizing, 15, 27
  basic techniques, 22
  application, 8
  merging, 27
  Microsoft, 8, 22
  moving, 17
  shutting down, 20,21
  starting Excel for. 25
Write, 19
  program icon, 13

Zooming views. 24

118